Fetch the key facts with CGP!

Quick question — have you memorised the facts in CGP's Knowledge Organiser for AQA GCSE Geography?

You have? Great! Now you can use this Knowledge Retriever to check you've really got everything stuck in your brain.

There are memory tests for each topic, plus mixed quiz questions to make extra sure you've really remembered all the vital facts. Enjoy.

CGP — still the best! ☺

Our sole aim here at CGP is to produce the highest quality books — carefully written, immaculately presented and dangerously close to being funny.

Then we work our socks off to get them out to you — at the cheapest possible prices.

Contents

How to Use This Book.................................2

Unit 1 — Living with the Physical Environment

Section A — The Challenge of Natural Hazards

Natural Hazards.................................3

Tectonic Plates.................................5

Tectonic Hazards.................................7

Mixed Practice Quizzes.................................11

Global Atmospheric Circulation.................................13

Tropical Storms.................................15

UK Weather Hazards.................................17

Mixed Practice Quizzes.................................19

Climate Change.................................21

Mixed Practice Quizzes.................................25

Section B — The Living World

Ecosystems.................................27

Tropical Rainforests.................................29

Tropical Rainforests — Deforestation.................................31

Tropical Rainforests and Sustainability.................................33

Mixed Practice Quizzes.................................35

Hot Deserts.................................37

The Sahara and Desertification.................................39

Mixed Practice Quizzes.................................41

Polar and Tundra Environments.................................43

Alaska and Sustainable Management.................................45

Mixed Practice Quizzes.................................47

Section C — Physical Landscapes in the UK

The UK Physical Landscape.................................49

Coastal Processes.................................51

Coastal Landforms.................................53

Coastal Management.................................55

Mixed Practice Quizzes.................................57

The River Valley and Fluvial Processes.................................59

River Landforms.................................61

Mixed Practice Quizzes.................................65

Flooding and Flood Management.................................67

Mixed Practice Quizzes.................................71

Glacial Processes.................................73

Glacial Landforms.................................75

Land Use in Glacial Landscapes.................................77

Mixed Practice Quizzes.................................79

Unit 2 — Challenges in the Human Environment

Section A — Urban Issues and Challenges

Urban Growth.................................81

Urban Growth — Lagos.................................83

UK Cities.................................85

Sustainable Urban Living.................................89

Mixed Practice Quizzes.................................91

Section B — The Changing Economic World

Measuring Development.................................93

Uneven Development 97

Reducing the Global Development Gap 99

Mixed Practice Quizzes 101

Economic Development in India 103

Economic Development in the UK 107

Mixed Practice Quizzes 111

Section C — The Challenge of Resource Management

Resources — Globally and in the UK 113

Food Supply and Demand 117

Increasing Food Production 119

Sustainable Food Supply 121

Mixed Practice Quizzes 123

Water Supply and Demand 125

Increasing Water Supply 127

Sustainable Water Supply 129

Mixed Practice Quizzes 131

Energy Supply and Demand 133

Increasing Energy Supplies 135

Sustainable Energy 137

Mixed Practice Quizzes 139

Geographical Applications & Skills

Geographical Applications

Fieldwork 141

Geographical Skills

Maps 143

Charts and Graphs 149

Statistics 153

Mixed Practice Quizzes 155

Camouflage Champions 157

Acknowledgements 158

Published by CGP.
Based on the classic CGP style created by Richard Parsons.

Editors: Claire Boulter, Tom Carney, Katherine Faudemer, Sharon Keeley-Holden, Becca Lakin.
Contributor: Paddy Gannon.

With thanks to Karen Wells for the proofreading.
With thanks to Lottie Edwards for the copyright research.

ISBN: 978 1 78908 722 2

Printed by Elanders Ltd, Newcastle upon Tyne.
Clipart from Corel®

How to Use This Book

Every page in this book has a matching page in the GCSE Geography **Knowledge Organiser**.
Before using this book, try to **memorise** everything on a Knowledge Organiser page.
Then follow these **seven steps** to see how much knowledge you're able to retrieve...

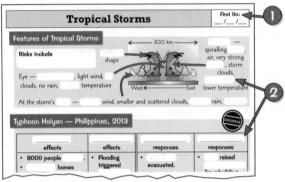

1 In this book, there are two versions of each page. Find the **'First Go'** of the page you've tried to memorise, and write the **date** at the top.

2 Use what you've learned from the Knowledge Organiser to **fill in** any dotted lines or white spaces.

⎍⎍⎍ You may need to draw, complete or add labels to diagrams too. ⎍⎍⎍

3 Use the Knowledge Organiser to **check your work**.
Use a **different coloured pen** to write in anything you missed or that wasn't quite right. This lets you see clearly what you **know** and what you **don't know**.

4 After doing the First Go page, **wait a few days**. This is important because **spacing out** your retrieval practice helps you to remember things better.

5 Now do the **Second Go** page.

⎍⎍⎍ The Second Go page is harder — it has more things missing. ⎍⎍⎍

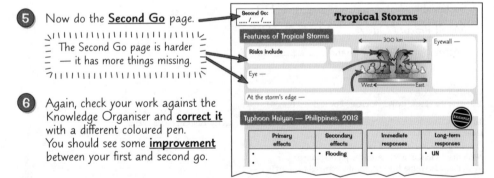

6 Again, check your work against the Knowledge Organiser and **correct it** with a different coloured pen.
You should see some **improvement** between your first and second go.

7 **Wait** another few days, then try recreating the whole Knowledge Organiser page on a **blank piece of paper**. If you can do this, you'll know you've **really learned it**.

There are also **Mixed Practice Quizzes** dotted throughout the book:
- The quizzes come in sets of four. They test a mix of content from the previous few pages.
- Do each quiz on a different day — write the date you do each one at the top of the quiz.
- Tick the questions you get right and record your score in the box at the end.

Natural Hazards

First Go:
..... / ..... / .....

Two Types of Natural Hazard

NATURAL HAZARD — natural process which can threaten _____ .

1 _____ hazards — caused by land / tectonic processes, e.g. _____ .

2 Meteorological hazards — caused by _____ , e.g. _____ .

Three Hazard Risk Factors

HAZARD RISK — the probability of people being _____ .

1 Vulnerability: More people in a hazardous area. ➡ _____

2 Capacity to Cope: More developed areas have _____ . ➡ Lower risk

3 Nature of Hazard:

- Type — some hazards can be _____ / monitored. ➡ _____
- Magnitude — _____ hazards have greater effects. ➡ Higher risk
- _____ — some hazards occur more often. ➡ Higher risk

Effects

Primary effects → _____ _____ caused by hazards. E.g.

- Deaths _____
- Buildings _____
- _____ water supplies
- Damaged _____
- Damaged _____

Secondary effects happen _____ , often as a result of _____ . E.g.

- Other hazards, e.g. _____
- _____ from poor sanitation
- Shortages of _____
- _____ economy

Responses

_____ happen just before, during or right after a hazard. E.g.

- _____ people
- Seek / send _____
- Provide _____
- _____ injured
- Supply temporary _____

Long-term responses deal with _____ . E.g.

- _____ people
- _____ water / gas / electricity
- Boost _____ , e.g. with tourism
- Improve _____

4

Natural Hazards

Two Types of Natural Hazard

NATURAL HAZARD —

1 Geological hazards —

2 Meteorological hazards —

Three Hazard Risk Factors

HAZARD RISK —

1 Vulnerability: ➡️

2 Capacity to Cope: ➡️

3 Nature of Hazard:
- Type — ➡️
- ➡️ Higher risk
- Frequency — ➡️

Effects

Primary effects →

- Deaths
-
-
- Damaged
- Damaged

Secondary effects happen

- Other
-
- Shortages
-

Responses

Immediate responses happen

-
-
- Provide
-
- Supply

Long-term responses deal with

-
- Restore
-
- Improve

Unit 1A — The Challenge of Natural Hazards

 ☑ ☑ ☑

Tectonic Plates

Tectonic Plates

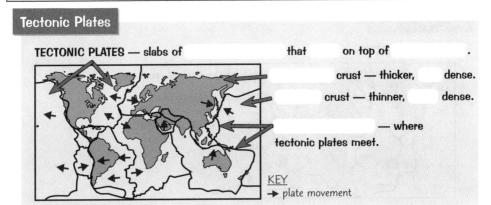

TECTONIC PLATES — slabs of ⬜ that ⬜ on top of ⬜.

⬜ crust — thicker, ⬜ dense.

⬜ crust — thinner, ⬜ dense.

⬜ — where tectonic plates meet.

KEY
→ plate movement

Three Types of Plate Margin

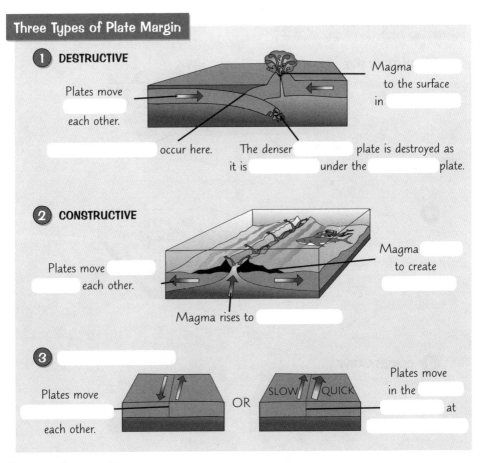

1 DESTRUCTIVE

Plates move ⬜ each other.

⬜ occur here.

Magma ⬜ to the surface in ⬜

The denser ⬜ plate is destroyed as it is ⬜ under the ⬜ plate.

2 CONSTRUCTIVE

Plates move ⬜ each other.

Magma rises to ⬜

Magma ⬜ to create ⬜

3 ⬜

Plates move ⬜ each other.

OR SLOW QUICK

Plates move in the ⬜ ⬜ at ⬜

 ☑ ☑ ☑

Tectonic Plates

Tectonic Plates

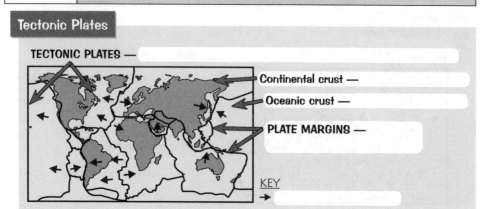

TECTONIC PLATES —

Continental crust —

Oceanic crust —

PLATE MARGINS —

KEY

Three Types of Plate Margin

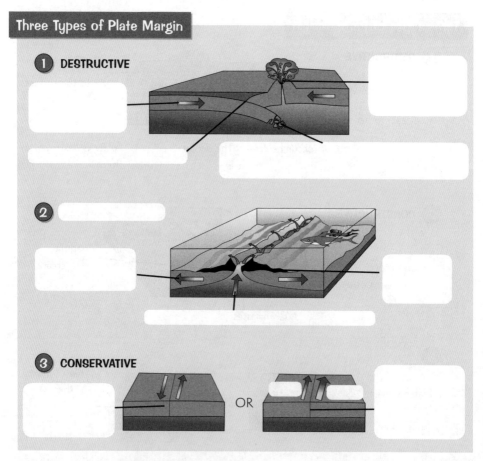

1 DESTRUCTIVE

2

3 CONSERVATIVE

OR

Unit 1A — The Challenge of Natural Hazards

Tectonic Hazards

Volcanoes

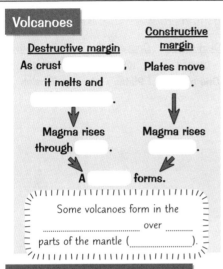

Destructive margin

As crust [____], it melts and [_____].

Magma rises through [____].

A [____] forms.

Constructive margin

Plates move [____].

Magma rises [____].

Some volcanoes form in the [................] over [........] parts of the mantle ([................]).

Earthquakes

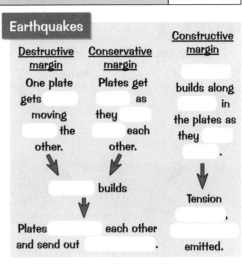

Destructive margin

One plate gets [____] moving [____] the other.

[____] builds

Plates [____] each other and send out [____].

Conservative margin

Plates get [____] as they [____] each other.

Constructive margin

builds along [____] in the plates as they [____].

Tension [____],

[____] emitted.

Living With Tectonic Hazards

People live in areas [____] to tectonic [____] for many reasons:

- They can't [____] to move.
- They [____] the risks.
- They've always [_____].

- They think the [____] will support them.
- [____] can minimise risk.
- Volcanic ash [_____].
- Volcanoes attract [____] creating [____].

Management Strategies

Monitoring and Prediction	[................] • Scientists monitor changes in [____] shape, escaping gas and small [____] • Helps predict [____].	[................] [____] and lasers monitor tectonic plate movements → [____].
Protection	• [____] / sloped [____] to withstand ash fall. • Trenches or barriers built to [____].	• New buildings use [____]. • [____] reinforce existing structures. • Automatic [____] for gas and electricity [____].
Planning	• [____] how to [____] if a hazard occurs. • Plan [____]. • [____] emergency supplies (e.g. [____], [____], [____]). • Avoid [____] in high-risk areas. • [____] practise [____] procedures.	

Second Go: ..... /..... /.....	**Tectonic Hazards**

Volcanoes

Destructive margin

As crust

Constructive margin

Plates

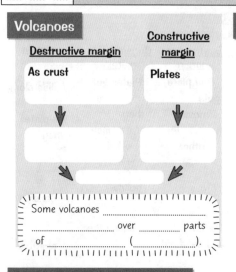

Some volcanoes .... over .... parts of .... (....................).

Earthquakes

Destructive margin

One plate

Conservative margin

Plates

Constructive margin

Tension builds

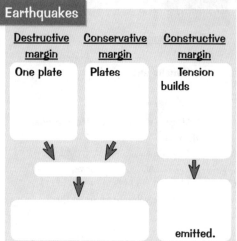

emitted.

Living With Tectonic Hazards

People live in areas vulnerable to tectonic hazards for many reasons:

- They can't
- They don't
- They've

- They think
-
-
-

Management Strategies

	Volcanoes	Earthquakes
Monitoring and Prediction	• Scientists monitor • Helps	Seismometers and
Protection	• Strengthened / • Trenches or	• New buildings • • Automatic
Planning	• Teach people • Plan • • Avoid •	

Tectonic Hazards

Effects of Two Earthquakes

Both earthquakes ....

	Kaikoura, ..., ... (HIC)	Gorkha, ..., ... (LIC)
Primary effects	• deaths, injured. • US $ billion . • 60 people → . • Roads and railways . • , and cut off.	• deaths, injured. • US $ billion • 800 000 . • 4 million people . • destroyed. • without clean water.
Secondary effects	• 100 000 blocked . • Clarence River blocked — . • with waves.	• Everest → killed. • Landslides roads which . • outbreaks killed.

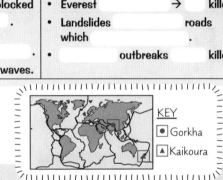

KEY
- ● Gorkha
- ▲ Kaikoura

Responses to Two Earthquakes

	Kaikoura, ..., ... , (HIC)	Gorkha, ..., ... (LIC)
Immediate responses	• issued. • Hundreds in . • Vulnerable people by . • Power within . • Temporary set up. • Other countries send .	• Efforts to people by . • Bodies and injured people . • housed in emergency shelters. • provided aid, but delivery was by roads.
Long-term responses	• $ million from for repairs and rebuilding. • reopened within years. • set up to provide . • Earthquake-proof laid.	• from World Bank Group. • Some roads . • Heritage sites reopened in to . • restored but . • NGOs working with residents to

 ☑ ☑ ☑

Tectonic Hazards

Effects of Two Earthquakes

....

	................., New Zealand, 2016 (.......)	................., Nepal, 2015 (.......)
Primary effects	• • US $ • • Roads and railways • Water	• • US $ • • Roads and bridges •
Secondary effects	• • Clarence River • Tsunami	• • Landslides • Typhus

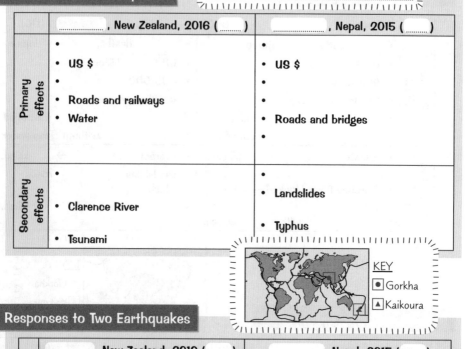

KEY
◉ Gorkha
▲ Kaikoura

Responses to Two Earthquakes

	................., New Zealand, 2016 (.......)	................., Nepal, 2015 (.......)
Immediate responses	• • Hundreds • • Power restored within • • Other countries	• • Bodies recovered and • • Charities
Long-term responses	• • Road and rail routes • Relief fund •	• • Some roads reopened • • Water supplies • NGOs

 ☑ ☑ ☑

Mixed Practice Quizzes

Phew — you've made it through p.3-10. Now you can manage the effect of your revision by answering these questions. Don't forget to add up your score at the end.

Quiz 1   Date: ...... / ...... / ......

1) True or false? More developed areas with better resources will have a higher hazard risk.
2) Give two plate movements that can happen at conservative plate margins.
3) Describe how earthquakes happen at conservative plate margins.
4) What is a 'natural hazard'?
5) Give one strategy that can help to protect people from earthquakes.
6) Give two long-term responses to the 2015 earthquake in Gorkha, Nepal.
7) True or false? Volcanic ash makes soil infertile.
8) Give three things that people might stockpile to prepare for natural hazards.
9) True or false? People choose to live in areas vulnerable to natural hazards.
10) What is the difference between continental crust and oceanic crust?

Total:

Quiz 2   Date: ...... / ...... / ......

1) What name is given to the boundary where tectonic plates meet?
2) What is the difference between an immediate response and a long-term response? Give one example of each.
3) Give one way that buildings can be protected from volcanic eruptions.
4) What happens when stuck plates jerk free at destructive plate margins?
5) As a long term response, why might governments encourage tourists to visit their country after a natural disaster?
6) Describe the movement of plates at destructive plate margins.
7) Give two primary effects of the 2016 earthquake in Kaikoura, New Zealand.
8) Give two things that scientists can monitor to help predict volcanic eruptions.
9) How can trenches and barriers protect settlements from volcanic eruptions?
10) True or false? Earthquakes can happen at all types of plate margin.

Total:

Mixed Practice Quizzes

Quiz 3 Date: ...... / ...... / ......

1) What happens to oceanic crust at destructive margins?
2) Give two immediate responses to the 2016 earthquake in Kaikoura.
3) What is meant by 'hazard risk'?
4) Where do hotspots typically form?
5) What can scientists use to monitor tectonic plate movements?
6) Describe how earthquakes happen at destructive plate margins.
7) Describe the damage caused by the:
   a) 2016 earthquake in Kaikoura, New Zealand.
   b) 2015 earthquake in Gorkha, Nepal.
8) Give three ways that areas can plan for natural hazards.
9) a) What is a 'primary effect'? Give an example.
   b) What is a 'secondary effect'? Give an example.
10) Describe how volcanoes form at constructive plate margins.

Total:

Quiz 4 Date: ...... / ...... / ......

1) How can the frequency of a hazard affect hazard risk?
2) What is a 'hotspot'?
3) Give three reasons why people live in areas vulnerable to tectonic hazards.
4) Name two types of tectonic hazard.
5) Give two secondary effects of the 2015 earthquake in Gorkha, Nepal.
6) After the 2015 earthquake, how much aid did the World Bank Group send to Gorkha, Nepal?
7) True or false? Volcanoes can be tourist attractions.
8) Name the two types of plate margin where volcanoes can form.
9) a) Give the magnitude of the 2016 earthquake in Kaikoura, New Zealand.
   b) Give the magnitude of the 2015 earthquake in Gorkha, Nepal.
10) Where do ocean trenches form?

Total:

Global Atmospheric Circulation

Global Atmospheric Circulation Model

KEY ● Low Pressure Belt ● High Pressure Belt

GLOBAL ATMOSPHERIC CIRCULATION —
the transfer of [____] from the
to the [____] by the movement of [____].

Sun [____] equator. Air [____],
forming a [____],
then [____] and moves away.

At 30° N and S, cool air [____],
creating a [____].
It moves back towards [____]
([____] winds) or towards
the [____] ([____]).

At 60° N and S, [____] surface
air rises, creating [____] pressure.
Some air moves [____].
The rest moves [____].

At the [____], [____] air sinks and creates [____]
pressure. Air flows [____] equator.

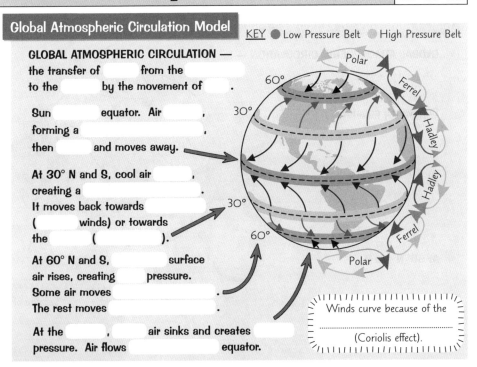

Winds curve because of the
....
(Coriolis effect).

Weather Impacts

Equator:
[____] directly overhead →
Warm, [____] air rises →

[____] N and S:
Moisture [____]
released → [____] rainfall

[____] N and S:
[____] rising air →

Atmospheric Circulation and Tropical Storm Formation

TROPICAL STORMS — [____] systems with intense [____] and [____].

• Between [____] and [____] N and S   • Sea temperature [____]   • Low wind [____]

Warm water [____],
[____] and [____],
producing [____].
→ drives [____]

[____] pressure [____] winds
move tropical storms [____].

Storms [____]
as they move over [____] water.

[____] makes storms rotate.   Storms [____] energy moving over [____] / cold water.

 ☑   ☑   ☺ ☑

Unit 1A — The Challenge of Natural Hazards

Global Atmospheric Circulation

Global Atmospheric Circulation Model

KEY ● Low Pressure Belt ● High Pressure Belt

GLOBAL ATMOSPHERIC CIRCULATION —

Sun warms equator.

At 30° N and S,

At 60° N and S,

At the poles,

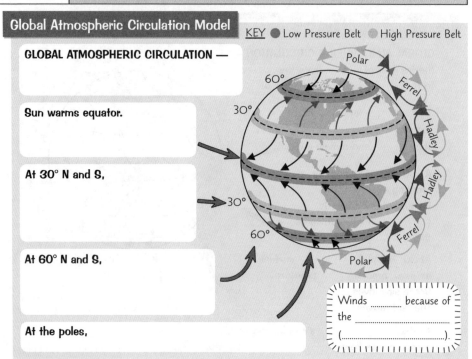

Winds .... because of the .... (......................................).

Weather Impacts

Equator:	30° N and S:	60° N and S:

Atmospheric Circulation and Tropical Storm Formation

TROPICAL STORMS —

- Between
- Sea
-

| Warm water evaporates, | → | Low pressure | → | | → | |

.... effect ....

.... lose energy ....

Unit 1A — The Challenge of Natural Hazards

Tropical Storms

Features of Tropical Storms

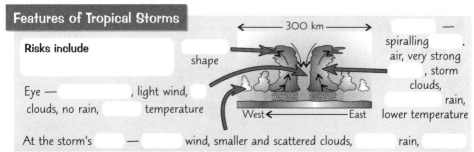

Risks include _____

_____ shape

Eye — _____, light wind, _____ clouds, no rain, _____ temperature

At the storm's _____ — _____ wind, smaller and scattered clouds, _____ rain, _____

← 300 km →

West ← → East

spiralling _____ air, very strong _____, storm clouds, _____ rain, lower temperature

Typhoon Haiyan — Philippines, 2013

EXAMPLE

...... effects	...... effects	...... responses	...... responses
• 8000 people _____. • _____ homes severely _____. • _____ lines destroyed. • Water _____. • _____ hectares of farmland _____.	• Flooding triggered _____. • _____ jobs lost. • Outbreaks of _____ e.g. dysentery.	• _____ evacuated. • Charities gave _____, _____ and clean water. • _____ built for _____ people.	• _____ raised for rebuilding. • Storm-resistant _____ built. • _____ urged to visit.

Flooding / deaths caused by ....

Reducing Tropical Storm Effects

Prediction and Monitoring	....	Protection
• _____, _____ and _____ monitor storms. • _____ predict storm paths.	• Future developments _____. • _____ planned. • Emergency services practise _____.	• Buildings designed to _____. • Buildings _____. • _____ built.

Climate Change and Tropical Storms

Distribution: _____ above 27 °C ⟹ Tropical storms at _____

_____ Oceans above 27 °C _____ ⟹ More time for tropical storms to form

Intensity: More evaporation and _____ ⟹ More _____ tropical storms

 ☑ ☑ ☑

Second Go:
..... / ..... / .....

Tropical Storms

Features of Tropical Storms

Risks include

Eye —

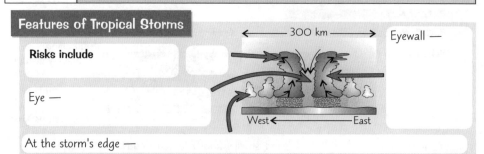

← 300 km →

Eyewall —

West ← → East

At the storm's edge —

Typhoon Haiyan — Philippines, 2013

EXAMPLE

Primary effects	Secondary effects		Immediate responses	Long-term responses
•	• Flooding		•	• UN
•			• Charities	
• Electricity	•			•
• Water	• Outbreaks		• Pit latrines	• Tourists
•				

Reducing Tropical Storm Effects

Prediction and Monitoring	Planning	Protection
•	•	• Buildings
• Computer	•	•
	• Emergency	•

Climate Change and Tropical Storms

Distribution: ⟹

Frequency: ⟹

Intensity: ⟹

  ✓ ✓ ✓

UK Weather Hazards

Types of UK Weather Hazards

Strong	.... damage. .... disruption. .... trees and .... can kill people.
Heavy	.... damages homes, disrupts transport and can .... people. Recovery ....
Snow and	People .... ice or die from ....
....	.... failure. Rules introduced ....
Thunderstorms	.... (see above). .... can cause fires.
.... waves	.... builds up. People suffer from .... or breathing difficulties. Roads .... and rails .... Tourism may ....

Extreme Weather

The UK's weather is becoming ....

Seven of eleven .... on record occurred since ....

.... — .... month in ....

Ten .... all since ....

.... — Many .... records broken.

Major .... events .... over the past ....

Somerset Levels Flooding — Dec. 2013-Feb. 2014

Causes	Impacts	Management
Physical: • .... during winter 2013-2014. • Rain fell on .... , ... ground. • .... and .... **Human:** • Rivers hadn't been .... for	**Social:** • .... homes flooded. • Villages .... • Transport links .... • .... prices soared. **Economic:** • .... damage. • Businesses lost .... • .... lost. **Environmental:** • .... flooded. • Crops destroyed. • .... made ground toxic. • Loss of .... • .... damaged vegetation.	**Before:** • People told to find emergency .... • .... and .... protected homes. **After:** • .... to: • Make .... permanent. • Regularly .... rivers .... and .... • .... River Sowy and King's Sedgemoor Drain. • Build .... at Bridgwater.

18

UK Weather Hazards

Types of UK Weather Hazards

Strong winds	Property Uprooted
Heavy rainfall	Flooding Recovery
Snow and ice	People
Drought	Crop
Thunderstorms	Strong
Heat waves	Pollution

Extreme Weather

Dec. 2010 —

Ten

2010-2014 —

Major flooding

Somerset Levels Flooding — Dec. 2013-Feb. 2014

Causes	Impacts	Management
Physical: • • Rain fell • Human: • Rivers	Social: • • Villages • Transport • Economic: • • Local • Environmental: • • Crops • • • Mud	Before: • People • After: Flood Action Plan. £ • Make • • Widen •

Mixed Practice Quizzes

Wow, you stormed through p.13-18. You can monitor what you remember by circulating through these quizzes. No doubt they'll give you a surge in confidence.

Quiz 1   Date: ...... / ...... / ......

1) Give three factors that contribute to the formation of tropical storms.
2) True or false? Evaporation influences the power of tropical storms.
3) What happens to warm air at the equator?
4) Give two primary effects of Typhoon Haiyan.
5) Give two management strategies that were implemented as part of the Flood Action Plan after the Somerset Levels Flooding.
6) What causes tropical storms to rotate?
7) What industry might benefit from a heat wave?
8) Describe the conditions in the eye of a tropical storm.
9) Give two economic impacts of the Somerset Levels Flooding.
10) True or false? The path of a tropical storm can be predicted.

Total:

Quiz 2   Date: ...... / ...... / ......

1) What is a 'tropical storm'?
2) a) Explain why the weather near the equator is hot.
   b) Explain why the weather near the equator is rainy.
3) Why does moving over land cause tropical storms to lose their energy?
4) Why might tropical storms start to form at higher latitudes?
5) Give two secondary effects of Typhoon Haiyan.
6) What protective measures were taken before the Somerset Levels Flooding happened?
7) What is global atmospheric circulation?
8) Name three types of UK weather hazards. Give an impact of each one.
9) Give one social, one economic and one environmental impact of the Somerset Levels Flooding.
10) How can buildings be protected from tropical storms?

Total:

Mixed Practice Quizzes

Quiz 3 Date: ...... / ...... / ......

1) What is the difference between trade winds and westerlies?
2) Describe how tropical storms form.
3) True or false? The UK's weather is becoming less extreme.
4) How can drought affect crops?
5) Give two characteristics of a tropical storm's eyewall.
6) True or false? Major flooding events have become more frequent in the UK over the past decade.
7) Give two immediate responses to Typhoon Haiyan.
8) Name three characteristics of thunderstorms.
9) How did human activity contribute to the Somerset Levels Flooding?
10) How might climate change affect the frequency of tropical storms?

Total:

Quiz 4 Date: ...... / ...... / ......

1) Give three risks associated with tropical storms.
2) Give two long-term responses to Typhoon Haiyan.
3) What were the physical causes of the Somerset Levels Flooding between December 2013 and February 2014?
4) Give two pieces of evidence that show the UK's weather is becoming more extreme.
5) How might climate change affect the intensity of tropical storms?
6) What happens to cool air when it reaches the poles?
7) Explain why the climate is dry at 30° N and S.
8) What is the weather like at the edge of a tropical storm?
9) What caused the flooding when Typhoon Haiyan made landfall?
10) What type of pressure belt forms at 60° N and S?

Total:

Climate Change

Evidence for Climate Change

CLIMATE CHANGE — any _____ in the Earth's climate _____ .

During the _____ period (the last _____ years), Earth has shifted between glacial periods (_____) and interglacial periods (_____).

.... cores	.... cores	.... rings	Pollen analysis	Temperature records
_____ trapped in layers of ice show temperature _____ .	Remains of _____ in sediments show _____ .	_____ rings mean _____ , conditions.	Preserved pollen shows _____ and _____ .	_____ measurements since _____ . _____ records extend further back.

Three Natural Causes

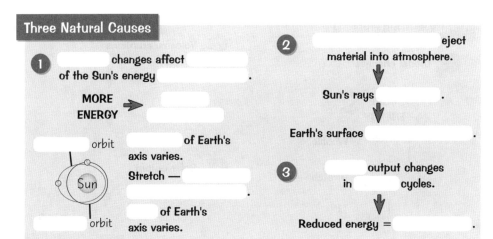

1 _____ changes affect _____ of the Sun's energy _____ .

MORE ENERGY ➤ _____

_____ orbit

Sun

_____ orbit

_____ of Earth's axis varies.

Stretch — _____ .

_____ of Earth's axis varies.

2 _____ eject material into atmosphere.

Sun's rays _____ .

Earth's surface _____ .

3 _____ output changes in _____ cycles.

Reduced energy = _____ .

Four Human Causes

_____ is the sharp rise in temp. over the last century.

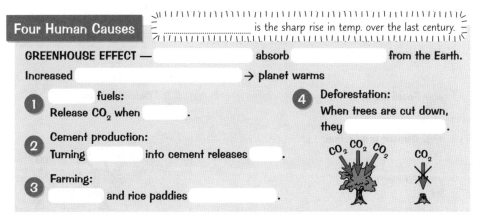

GREENHOUSE EFFECT — _____ absorb _____ from the Earth.

Increased _____ → planet warms

1 _____ fuels: Release CO_2 when _____ .

2 Cement production: Turning _____ into cement releases _____ .

3 Farming: _____ and rice paddies _____ .

4 Deforestation: When trees are cut down, they _____ .

CO_2 CO_2 CO_2 CO_2

Unit 1A — The Challenge of Natural Hazards

Climate Change

Evidence for Climate Change

CLIMATE CHANGE — _____

_____

During the _____ period (the last _____ years), Earth has shifted between _____ periods (_____) and interglacial periods (_____).

Ice cores	Sediment cores	Tree rings	Pollen analysis	Temperature records
Gases	Remains of	Thicker	Preserved	Accurate measurements

Three Natural Causes

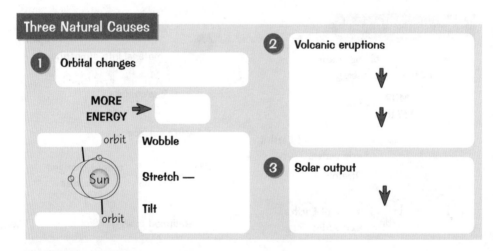

1 Orbital changes

MORE ENERGY →

_____ orbit

_____ orbit

Wobble

Stretch —

Tilt

Sun

2 Volcanic eruptions

3 Solar output

Four Human Causes

Global warming is _____

GREENHOUSE EFFECT — _____

_____ → _____

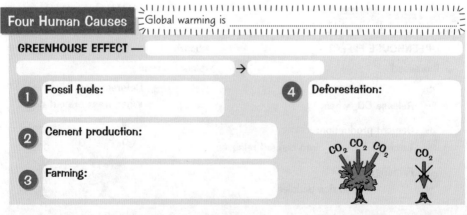

1 Fossil fuels:

2 Cement production:

3 Farming:

4 Deforestation:

CO_2 CO_2 CO_2 CO_2

Climate Change

Effects of Climate Change

Wet places will get .... Dry places will get ....

ENVIRONMENTAL	HUMAN
• .... and ice sheets .... → sea level	• More deaths ....
• .... sea ice → loss of	• Fewer deaths ....
• Flooding of .... , ... areas → loss of coastal habitats.	• People leave .... → .... in other areas.
• Changing	• Decreased rainfall in some areas → ....
• Species are .... , e.g. coral reefs	• .... → malnutrition, ill health and death.
• Species moving to	• .... crop yields may increase.
• .... making species extinct →	• .... → management / rebuilding costs rise.

Management Strategies

MITIGATION aims to .... of climate change.

Alternative .... :
.... or .... energy sources lower emissions.

Planting trees:
More trees = ...

Carbon Capture and Storage:
.... from .... stored securely.

International agreements:
.... (2016) — .... countries pledged to reduce ....

ADAPTATION .... of climate change.

Changing .... Systems:
• Plant crops suited to ....
• .... can create drought-resistant ....

Managing Water Supply:
• .... help limit water use.
• Rainwater and waste water ....

Coping with .... :
• Better .... and .... , e.g. Thames Barrier.
• Build houses on .... , build .... flood shelters.

Climate Change

Effects of Climate Change

.... places .... : .... places ....

ENVIRONMENTAL	HUMAN
•	• More
→ sea level rises.	•
• Shrinking	• People leave
→	→
•	• Decreased rainfall in some areas
→	→
• Changing precipitation patterns.	• Lower
• Species are declining	→
e.g.	
	•
•	
• Habitat damage	• More extreme weather
→	→

Management Strategies

MITIGATION

Alternative energy production:

Planting trees:

Carbon Capture and Storage:

International agreements:

ADAPTATION

Changing Agricultural Systems:
•

•

Managing Water Supply:
•

•

Coping with Rising Sea Levels:
•

•

 ✓ ✓ ✓

Mixed Practice Quizzes

You've almost reached the end of this section — hooray! Now use these quizzes to check how much you remember from p.21-24, then have a well-deserved lie-down.

Quiz 1 Date: ...... / ...... / ......

1) How can ice cores provide evidence for climate change?
2) Give two environmental effects of climate change.
3) How can climate change lead to overcrowding?
4) True or false? Glacial periods are colder than interglacial periods.
5) How are rising greenhouse gas emissions affecting the Earth's temperature?
6) What might happen to weather as a result of climate change?
7) How can buildings be constructed to cope with rising sea levels?
8) Give an example of an international agreement that aims to reduce climate change.
9) Explain why sea levels are rising and how this affects polar habitats.
10) How can cement production contribute to climate change?

Total:

Quiz 2 Date: ...... / ...... / ......

1) What is the 'greenhouse effect'?
2) How is mitigation different to adaptation when dealing with climate change?
3) Give a type of energy that can be used instead of fossil fuels.
4) a) How might climate change affect global crop yield?
   b) How might climate change affect crop yield at higher latitudes?
5) How can rain and waste water be used to help manage water supply?
6) What is Carbon Capture and Storage?
7) What happens when fossil fuels are burnt?
8) True or false? Planting trees releases more CO_2 into the atmosphere.
9) What is the name of the geological time period that spans the last 2.6 million years?
10) Explain how volcanic eruptions can affect the Earth's climate.

Total:

Mixed Practice Quizzes

Quiz 3   Date: ...... / ...... / ......

1) How can changes to the Earth's orbit contribute to climate change? ☑
2) Give two human effects of climate change. ☑
3) What sort of climate do thicker tree rings provide evidence of? ☑
4) What can be built to cope with rising sea levels? ☑
5) How can volcanic eruptions lead to the
   temporary cooling of the Earth's surface? ☑
6) How can biotechnology respond to the effects of climate change? ☑
7) How can changing precipitation patterns affect water availability? ☑
8) How does deforestation contribute to global warming? ☑
9) Which two characteristics of the Earth's axis vary as it orbits the sun? ☑
10) How might climate change cause biodiversity to decline? ☑

Total: ☐

Quiz 4   Date: ...... / ...... / ......

1) What gas do rice paddies emit? ☑
2) How might reduced solar output contribute to climate change? ☑
3) How far back do accurate temperature records extend? ☑
4) Give one thing that people can do to limit their water usage. ☑
5) True or false? Species are moving to lower latitudes
   in response to climate change. ☑
6) In general, what will happen to places that are
   wet if the climate continues to change? ☑
7) How can sediment cores provide evidence for climate change? ☑
8) The Earth's orbit around the Sun varies in shape from circular to what? ☑
9) Describe how analysing pollen can provide evidence for climate change. ☑
10) How might agricultural systems change in response to climate change? ☑

Total: ☐

Ecosystems

First Go:
..... /..... /.....

Key Definitions

ECOSYSTEM — All the [blank] and [blank] parts of an area.

- PRODUCERS produce [blank] from [blank].
- CONSUMERS eat [blank] for energy.
- DECOMPOSERS [blank] for energy.

Nutrient Cycle

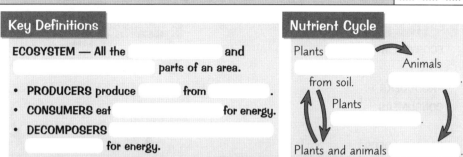

Plants [blank]   Animals

[blank] from soil.   [blank]

Plants [blank]   [blank]

Plants and animals [blank]

Small-scale Ecosystem — Slapton Ley Reed Beds, UK

EXAMPLE

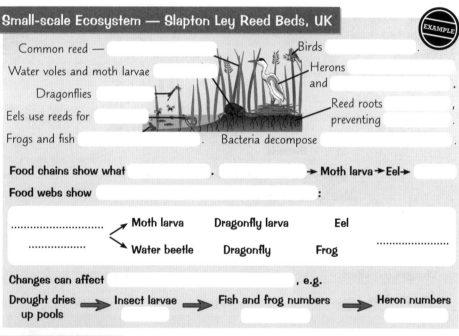

Common reed — [blank]   Birds [blank]

Water voles and moth larvae [blank]   Herons [blank] and [blank].

Dragonflies [blank]   Reed roots [blank] preventing [blank],

Eels use reeds for [blank]

Frogs and fish [blank].   Bacteria decompose [blank].

Food chains show what [blank].   → Moth larva → Eel →

Food webs show [blank]:

.... → Moth larva   Dragonfly larva   Eel

.... → Water beetle   Dragonfly   Frog   ....

Changes can affect [blank], e.g.

Drought dries up pools → Insect larvae [blank] → Fish and frog numbers [blank] → Heron numbers [blank]

Global Ecosystems

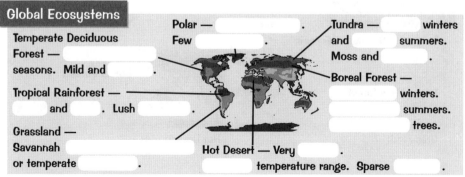

Temperate Deciduous Forest — [blank] seasons. Mild and [blank].

Tropical Rainforest — [blank] and [blank]. Lush [blank].

Grassland — Savannah [blank] or temperate [blank].

Polar — [blank]. Few [blank].

Hot Desert — Very [blank]. [blank] temperature range. Sparse [blank].

Tundra — [blank] winters and [blank] summers. Moss and [blank].

Boreal Forest — [blank] winters. [blank] summers. [blank] trees.

28

Ecosystems

Key Definitions

ECOSYSTEM —

PRODUCERS

CONSUMERS

DECOMPOSERS

Nutrient Cycle

Plants

Small-scale Ecosystem — Slapton Ley Reed Beds, UK

EXAMPLE

Common

Water voles and moth larvae

Birds

Herons nest in

Eels use

Frogs and fish

Reed roots bind

Bacteria

_____ show what _____ what. Common reed → _____ → Heron

_____ show how food chains _____.

Common reed

Changes can affect _____, e.g.

Drought dries
up pools → → →

Global Ecosystems

Temperate Deciduous Forest:

Polar:

Tundra:

Boreal Forest:

Tropical Rainforest:

Grassland:

Hot Desert:

Tropical Rainforests

Characteristics

Climate	No definite _____ . Sun _____ → _____ . High daily _____ .
Plants	Evergreen plants take advantage of _____ . Tall _____ and dense _____ → _____ . _____ grow on other plants.
Soil	Rain washes _____ → not very _____ . Fallen leaves _____ .
People	Indigenous people have _____ → _____ .
Animals	More _____ than any other _____ .

Rainforest animals: _____

Biodiversity

BIODIVERSITY — the _____ living in a particular area.

Constant _____ → _____ → Plants and animals _____ → _____
_____ _____ environment _____ biodiversity

But:
Deforestation / _____ → Change imposed on species → _____ → _____ of
_____ development who _____ of some species _____ biodiversity

Interdependence

Surface soil _____ in _____ . _____ affects ecosystem:

Warm / wet climate → fast _____ . Plants grow _____ . Trees _____ .

Plants / animals _____ . ← Animals _____ for nutrients. Soil _____ .

Rain _____ away.

Plants _____

Adaptations

ANIMALS
- Sharp sense of smell to cope with _____ .
- Nocturnal animals _____ to _____ .
- _____ help birds fly between _____ .
- Many animals can _____ to cross _____
- _____ to hide from _____ .

PLANTS
- Trees are _____ to reach _____ .
- _____ drip-tips for easy runoff.
- Lianas _____ trees for _____
- _____ roots support tall trees.

Trees _____
Main _____
_____
_____ layer

Tropical Rainforests

Characteristics

Climate	No definite . Sun High
Plants	Evergreen plants Tall trees Epiphytes
Soil	Rain washes Fallen
People	
Animals	More

Biodiversity

Rainforest animals: _____

BIODIVERSITY — the variety of _____ .

| Constant | ➡ | Productive | ➡ | Plants | ➡ | |

But:

| | / ➡ | Change imposed on | ➡ | | ➡ | |
| human development | | | | of some species | | |

Interdependence

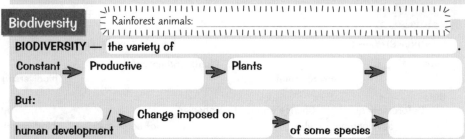

Surface _____

_____ climate   _____ easily.   Soil

→ fast _____ .

Plants / _____   ⬅ Animals eat _____ .   Plants

_____ affects ecosystem:

Adaptations

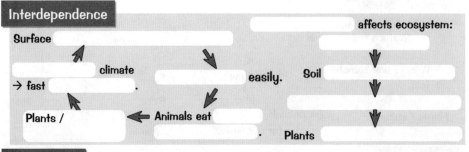

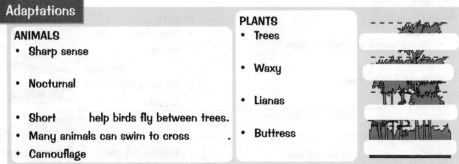

ANIMALS
* Sharp sense

* Nocturnal

* Short   help birds fly between trees.
* Many animals can swim to cross   .
* Camouflage

PLANTS
* Trees

* Waxy

* Lianas

* Buttress

Tropical Rainforests — Deforestation

 CASE STUDY

First Go: ..... / ..... / .....

Causes of Deforestation in The Amazon

Commercial Farming: _____ km² cleared to produce _____.
_____ cattle on 450 000 km² of pasture.

70-80%

20-25%

_____ **Farming:** Small-scale farmers grow _____ for _____.

Logging: _____ tempt _____ and _____ loggers.

2-3%   <2%

% of total deforestation in the Amazon.

Mineral Extraction:
Mining _____, _____ and _____
_____ boosts _____
_____ used.

Road Building:
_____ Highway
threatens to open up
_____.

Almost _____ hectares of forest were lost between 2001 and 2012.

Population _____:
_____ offered to _____
from _____

Energy Development:
_____ flooded
_____ km² of forest.

Three Impacts of Deforestation in the Amazon

1 CLIMATE CHANGE: _____ tonnes _____ stored in Amazon ➜ _____ releases _____ some of this as _____. ➜ Global _____

2 SOIL EROSION: _____ trees ➜ Less rain _____

Farmers clear _____ ⬆   Reduced soil _____ ⬅   More nutrients _____

3 ECONOMIC CHANGE:
• Loss of _____ → Brazilian rubber tappers _____.
• Buenaventura _____ (Peru) → _____ employees.
• Brazil exported $ _____ of _____ in March 2018.

Wealth and jobs boost _____ but can _____.

Changing Rates of Deforestation

Deforestation in Brazil _____ by _____ from 2004 to 2012.

Global _____ of _____ are _____ and generally _____, but some countries (e.g. _____) are trying to _____ this:

• Increased _____ reduces _____ for products from deforested areas.
• _____ Agreement — Brazil pledged to _____ by _____.
• _____ prevents large-scale _____.
• _____ now protects _____ of the Amazon.

CASE STUDY **Tropical Rainforests — Deforestation**

Causes of Deforestation in The Amazon

Commercial Farming: 250 00 km²

..................%

20-25%

Subsistence Farming:

Logging:

..................%

..................%

% of total deforestation in the Amazon.

Mineral Extraction:

Road Building:

Population Growth:

Energy Development:

Almost 18 million

Three Impacts of Deforestation in the Amazon

1 CLIMATE CHANGE: 140 billion   Felling

2 SOIL EROSION: Fewer → Less
Farmers ↑
← Reduced   More

3 ECONOMIC CHANGE:
• rubber trees →   lose jobs.
•   mining company (   )
Wealth and jobs ....
• Brazil exported

Changing Rates of Deforestation

Deforestation ....

Global rates of deforestation are

• Increased

• Paris

• Satellite

• Funding

Tropical Rainforests and Sustainability

Tropical Rainforests — Value

- Source of many _____ and _____ — some may still be _____.
- _____ development → _____ economic benefits (e.g. _____).
- Rainforests may _____ the _____ (trees _____).
- _____ of climate and _____ → deforestation _____ risk of drought or floods.

> Deforestation could affect _____ (e.g. _____) not just deforested areas.

Sustainable Management Strategies

SUSTAINABLE MANAGEMENT — getting the _____ we need _____ without _____ the _____ so that resources aren't _____ in the _____.

Replanting	• New _____ (of the _____) replace _____. • A legal requirement for _____ in certain countries.	
Selective Logging	• Some trees _____ but most _____. • Forest can _____.	Malaysia — _____ logging.
Ecotourism	• _____ groups of _____ follow _____ rules. • _____ hired → _____ for them to _____, _____ or _____ for income. • Incentive to _____.	_____ of Costa Rica protected from _____ for ecotourism.
Education	• Encourages _____ product use. • Teaches locals to make _____ in an _____.	_____ teaches communities in _____ about _____ living.
Conservation	• _____ / nature reserves restrict _____. • Countries can _____ for _____ to donate to.	2018 — _____ paid _____ into Brazil's _____ Fund.
Reducing Debt	• Debt can be _____ — countries _____ to log, farm or mine _____ it. • _____ swaps → country's debt _____ if _____ is guaranteed.	2011 — USA reduced _____ debt by _____.
International Hardwood Agreements	• Prevent _____ logging. • Promote the use of _____ from _____-managed forests.	Forest Stewardship Council® _____ on sustainably-sourced _____.

Second Go: ..... / ..... /	# Tropical Rainforests and Sustainability

Tropical Rainforests — Value

- Source of many products and
- _____ development → long-term
- Rainforests may
- Regulation of _____ → deforestation increases risk of

Deforestation could affect
....
....

Sustainable Management Strategies

SUSTAINABLE MANAGEMENT — getting the _____
damaging the environment so that _____ .

Replanting	• New • A legal requirement for	
Selective Logging	• Some trees • Forest	— helicopter logging.
Ecotourism	• Small groups of • Locals • Incentive	21% of
Education	• Encourages • Teaches locals to	Rainforest Alliance teaches communities in
Conservation	• National parks / • Countries can set up	2018 —
Reducing Debt	• Debt can be cancelled • Conservation swaps →	2011 —
International Hardwood Agreements	• Prevent • Promote the use of hardwood from	Forest Stewardship Council®

Mixed Practice Quizzes

Now for the quick fire rounds on Ecosystems & Tropical Rainforests. They'll check if you've really got a grip on p.27-34. Mark each test yourself and tot up your score.

Quiz 1

Date: ...... / ...... / ......

1) What is a biotic part of an ecosystem?
2) Name four rainforest animals.
3) How do the nutrients animals eat return to the soil?
4) What is shown by a food web?
5) Explain how rainforests benefit the environment on a global scale.
6) In which global ecosystem are coniferous trees plentiful.
7) Why are tropical rainforests so hot?
8) Explain why the constant climate of tropical rainforests results in high biodiversity.
9) Give one adaptation that might benefit birds living in a tropical rainforest.
10) What causes most deforestation in the Amazon?

Total:

Quiz 2

Date: ...... / ...... / ......

1) How does a producer get energy?
2) Give two characteristics of a temperate deciduous forest.
3) Give two aims of international hardwood agreements.
4) What is the trend for global rates of deforestation?
5) Apart from farming and logging, give three causes of deforestation in the Amazon.
6) Give two adaptations that might benefit plants in a tropical rainforest.
7) Explain why deforestation results in a reduction of biodiversity.
8) What does a food chain show?
9) Define 'biodiversity'.
10) Roughly what area of the Amazon Rainforest has been cleared to grow soy?

Total:

Mixed Practice Quizzes

Quiz 3 | Date: ...... / ...... / ......

1) Give one negative economic impact that deforestation has had in the Amazon.

2) What is an abiotic part of an ecosystem?

3) Name the seven global ecosystems.

4) What is subsistence farming?

5) Why are tropical rainforest plants typically evergreen?

6) Why is a good sense of smell beneficial to animals living in a tropical rainforest?

7) Give two ways that Brazil is trying to reduce the rate of deforestation.

8) Explain how ecotourism can reduce deforestation in an area.

9) Define 'sustainable management'.

10) For a small scale ecosystem, such as a reed bed, explain how one change can affect consumers at different levels of the food chain.

Total:

Quiz 4 | Date: ...... / ...... / ......

1) True or false? Organic matter (e.g. fallen leaves) decomposes slowly in the Amazon Rainforest.

2) Helicopter logging is carried out in Malaysia. Which sustainable management strategy is this an example of?

3) How do consumers get energy?

4) Name the two types of grassland.

5) True or false? Tundra is characterised by a mild, damp climate.

6) Why do many rainforest plants have waxy drip-tips?

7) Give an example of how an energy-producing development caused deforestation in the Amazon.

8) Explain how deforestation can reduce soil fertility in the Amazon.

9) How can reducing debt encourage sustainable rainforest management?

10) Give two ways tropical rainforests can benefit humans on a global scale.

Total:

Hot Deserts

First Go:
..... /..... /.....

Characteristics

Climate	_____ rainfall. _____ clouds → extreme _____ (day) and extreme _____ (night).
Plants	Low _____ → _____ plants. Plants don't need much _____, e.g. _____. Plants are usually _____. Short _____ → quick _____ after rain.
Soil	Lack of _____ → low _____. _____ rainfall → _____. Shallow and _____
People	Live near _____ to grow _____. Nomadic → _____ for food / water.
Animals	_____ to harsh environment. Most mammals are _____ and _____. Most birds _____ during _____ conditions.

Deserts get _____ of rain per year.

Biodiversity

_____ biodiversity overall.
People threaten biodiversity:
- Desertification.
- Over-use and _____ of water supplies.
- Roads _____ → _____ animals threatened.
- Global warming makes deserts _____ → species _____ or risk _____ and _____.

Deserts contain biodiversity _____ — places with _____ proportions of endemic species at risk of extinction.

Interdependence

Hot, _____ climate → high _____ and little _____.
_____ animals Soil _____ and to _____. low in _____.
Low-density _____ ← Limited _____ growth → low _____.
Human _____ affects fragile _____:
cattle → soil _____.
_____ soil → sand forms _____.
Rainfall _____ → water supplies _____.
People, plants and animals _____.

Adaptations

PLANTS
- _____ roots reach deep _____ supplies.
- _____ roots absorb _____.
- _____ store water in large fleshy _____.
- _____ leaves, _____ and skin reduce _____.
- Some _____ only germinate after _____.

ANIMALS
- Nocturnal → avoid _____ temps.
- Long limbs and _____ ears increase _____ → helps _____ loss.
- _____ burrows → _____.
- _____ store _____ in fat (humps).
- Minimised _____ → kangaroo rats _____.

Hot Deserts

Characteristics

Climate	Very little
Plants	Low rainfall . Plants don't need much Plants are usually
Soil	Lack of leaf fall →
People	Live near
Animals	Adapted to harsh environment.

Deserts get ....

Biodiversity

Low ....

People   :

•

• Over-use

• Roads

• Global

Deserts contain ....

Interdependence

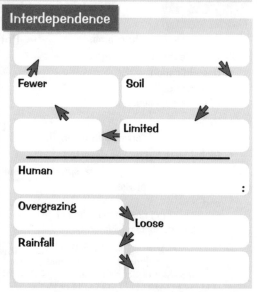

Fewer   Soil

Limited

Human   :

Overgrazing   Loose

Rainfall

Adaptations

PLANTS

• Long roots reach
• Wide roots
• Succulents

• Small
•
• Some seeds only germinate

ANIMALS

• Nocturnal →
• Long limbs and large

• Underground
• Camels store water in
• Minimised

The Sahara and Desertification

Opportunities and Challenges in the Sahara

CASE STUDY

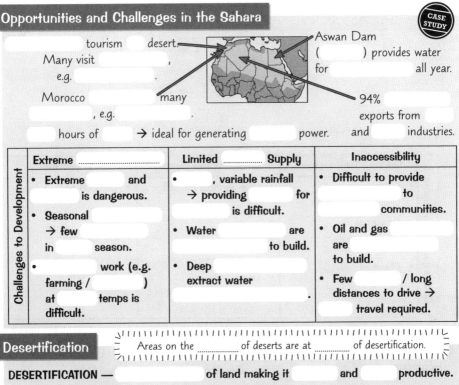

tourism   desert.
Many visit _____ ,
e.g. _____ .

Morocco _____ many
_____ , e.g. _____ .

_____ hours of _____ → ideal for generating _____ power.

Aswan Dam
(_____) provides water
for _____ all year.

94%
exports from
_____ and _____ industries.

	Extreme _____	Limited _____ Supply	Inaccessibility
Challenges to Development	• Extreme _____ and _____ is dangerous. • Seasonal _____ → few _____ in _____ season. • _____ work (e.g. farming / _____) at _____ temps is difficult.	• _____ , variable rainfall → providing _____ for _____ is difficult. • Water _____ are _____ to build. • Deep _____ extract water _____ .	• Difficult to provide _____ to _____ communities. • Oil and gas _____ are _____ to build. • Few _____ / long distances to drive → _____ travel required.

Desertification

Areas on the _____ of deserts are at _____ of desertification.

DESERTIFICATION — _____ of land making it _____ and _____ productive.

CAUSES:

Overgrazing:
Plants eaten _____
than they _____ .

Removal of fuel wood:
Trees _____ for _____
→ soil _____ .

Population growth:
Land _____
→ impacts _____ .

Over-cultivation:
Continually planting _____ in the _____
area _____ nutrients and _____ soil.

Climate Change:
Rising _____ increase evaporation
and decrease _____ → plants _____ .

REDUCING DESERTIFICATION RISK			
_____ management: • Grow crops that don't need much _____ , e.g. _____ . • _____ irrigation stops erosion.	**Tree** _____ : Trees act as _____ , shade crops and _____ sand.	_____ management: • _____ land between _____ / _____ to replenish _____ . • _____ crops so _____ nutrients are removed • _____ nutrients with compost.	_____ technology: Use _____ , sustainable, _____ materials, e.g. _____

Second Go: ..... / ..... / .....

The Sahara and Desertification

Opportunities and Challenges in the Sahara

CASE STUDY

Small-scale

Aswan

Morocco

94%

12+ →

	Extreme Temperatures	Limited Water Supply	Inaccessibility
Challenges to Development	• Extreme	• Low variable rainfall	• Difficult to
	• Seasonal	• Water	• Oil and gas
	• Physical	• Deep	• Few roads

Desertification

Areas on the edge

DESERTIFICATION — _____ of land making _____ and less _____ .

CAUSES:

Overgrazing:

Removal of fuel wood:

Population growth:

Over-cultivation:

Climate change:

REDUCING DESERTIFICATION RISK			
Water management:	**Tree planting:**	**Soil management:**	**Appropriate technology:**
• Grow	Trees	• Rest land	Use
		• Rotate	
• Drip		• Add nutrients with compost	

Unit 1B — The Living World

Mixed Practice Quizzes

Now to see how much you really know about hot deserts. Answer these questions based on p.37-40, then mark them yourself. Try not to get too hot under the collar.

Quiz 1
Date: ...... / ...... / ......

1) What is desertification?
2) How does road-building in the desert threaten biodiversity?
3) Why do deserts have low-density animal populations?
4) How much rainfall do hot deserts get every year?
5) Explain why long roots are beneficial for desert plants.
6) Hot deserts have over 12 hours of sun a day.
   How can this benefit humans?
7) True or false? Tourism is hugely popular in the middle of the Sahara Desert.
8) How can felling trees for fuel contribute to desertification?
9) Which areas of the desert are most at risk of desertification?
10) Why might desert industries struggle to operate continuously?

Total:

Quiz 2
Date: ...... / ...... / ......

1) Give two causes of desertification.
2) Name a type of irrigation that can reduce the risk of desertification.
3) What are biodiversity hotspots?
4) What is overgrazing?
5) Give one adaptation of desert plants that helps them
   absorb as much rainwater as possible.
6) True or false? Camels store water in their humps.
7) What is extracted from the Sahara desert in Morocco?
8) Appropriate technology solutions can reduce the risk of desertification.
   Describe the materials used in appropriate technology.
9) When are desert plants most likely to start their short life cycles?
10) How can long ears benefit animals that live in hot deserts?

Total:

Mixed Practice Quizzes

Quiz 3 Date: ...... / ...... / ......

1) Explain how planting trees can reduce the risk of desertification. ☑
2) Give two characteristics of animals found in the desert. ☑
3) Why is desert soil salty and low in nutrients? ☑
4) State three adaptations desert plants have to reduce transpiration. ☑
5) How does the Aswan Dam benefit Egypt? ☑
6) How might people living in the desert deal with the variable supply of food / water? ☑
7) Give two reasons why extreme heat presents a challenge to the development of the Sahara Desert. ☑
8) Why does population growth increase the risk of desertification? ☑
9) Describe an adaption that a named desert animal has to minimise water loss. ☑
10) How might desert animals respond to changes caused by global warming? ☑

Total: ☐

Quiz 4 Date: ...... / ...... / ......

1) What industries are responsible for almost all Algeria's exports? ☑
2) Explain why desert soil isn't very fertile. ☑
3) What effect does global warming have on hot deserts? ☑
4) Why do dust clouds increase the dryness of the desert? ☑
5) State an adaptation that many desert animals have which allows them to avoid the most intense desert heat. ☑
6) True or false? Drilling into the desert to extract water is sustainable. ☑
7) Give two reasons inaccessibility can pose a challenge to development in desert areas ☑
8) How can soil be managed to avoid nutrient depletion? ☑
9) In the desert, what do people tend to live near? ☑
10) Why do deserts experience extreme heat in the day but extreme cold at night? ☑

Total: ☐

Polar and Tundra Environments

Characteristics

.... areas can reach -90 °C. .... can reach -50 °C.

	Polar		Tundra	
Climate	Very _____ . Very low _____ . _____ but _____ seasons.		_____ . Low _____ . _____ but _____ seasons.	
Plants	_____ . Mosses and _____ Grasses on the _____ .		Hardy _____ , grasses, _____ , lichens. Small _____ trees in _____ areas.	
Soil	Covered by _____ → no exposed _____ .		Thin, _____ , _____ . Permafrost layer traps _____ .	
People	Mostly _____ .		_____ people. Oil & gas _____	
Animals	_____ bears, _____ , penguins.		Lemmings, _____ and _____ .	

Biodiversity

Very _____ biodiversity → Change in one _____ affects all _____ species.

Global _____ → some species move to _____ for _____ temps.

Some species can't go anywhere → Some _____ at risk of _____ or _____ .

Interdependence

Cold _____ decomposition. → Few _____ in _____ .

_____ plant growth.

follow herbivores.

Herbivores _____ to find _____ .

- Plants protect ....
- Permafrost gives plants ....

Cold environments are very _____ .

If people _____ plants, the exposed _____ is warmed by sun.

Permafrost may _____ & saturate soil → _____ gases released.

Plants can't _____ , herbivores struggle to find _____ .

Adaptations

PLANTS
- Plants become _____ to survive _____ and dark _____ .
- _____ -growing / _____ -shaped → _____ protection.
- Shallow _____ above _____ .
- Small _____ limit _____ .
- Short _____ season.

ANIMALS
- Fur or _____ keeps animals _____ .
- Animals _____ to conserve _____ .
- Non-hibernators → _____ to _____ on _____ food sources.
- Birds _____ to _____ areas for winter.
- _____ winter coats — help stalk prey, help prey _____ predators.

 ☑ ☑ ☑

Unit 1B — The Living World

Second Go:
..... / ..... / .....

Polar and Tundra Environments

Characteristics

Polar areas can reach .... Tundra can reach ....

	Polar	Tundra
Climate	Very	
Plants		Hardy
Soil	Covered	Thin Permafrost
People	Mostly	Oil and
Animals	Polar bears,	Lemmings

Biodiversity

Change in one → biodiversity

Global warming → Polar species → Some species

Interdependence

Cold → Few

Carnivores

Limited

Herbivores

• Plants ....
• Permafrost ....

Cold environments are very ....

If people trample plants the exposed

↓

Permafrost many melt &
soil → greenhouse

↓

Plants

Adaptations

PLANTS

• Plants

• Low

• Shallow

• Small

• Short

ANIMALS

• Fur or blubber

• Animals hibernate

• Non-hibernators → adapted

• Birds migrate to

• White winter coats — help

Alaska and Sustainable Management

Opportunities and Challenges in Alaska

Energy	Mineral resources	Fishing	Tourism
Oil and ____ — over ____ state's ____. Trans-Alaska ____ connects oil fields to ____.	Gold, ____, copper and ____ ore ____. $ ____ worth of ____ exported in ____.	2016 — fishing industry worth $ ____ and employed ____ fishermen.	2 ____ tourists bring in $ ____ each year and generate jobs for ____ people.

Inaccessibility:
- ____, ____ areas → difficult to ____.
- ____ travel → ____.
- Ice ____ → ____.
- Some ____ close in summer → ground too ____.
- Small, ____ population → far from ____ and ____.

Extreme Temperatures:
- Extreme ____ is ____
- ____ vary a lot.

Buildings and Infrastructure:
- ____ / ____ ground and extreme ____ makes construction expensive.
- ____ only happens in ____.
- Pipelines built on ____ to stop them ____.

Barrow, Alaska gets .... days of total .... a year.

Cold Environments — Value

WILDERNESS AREA — wild, ____ environments that are ____, uninhabited and ____.

They need to be ____ because:
- they provide ____ for organisms that can't ____ elsewhere.
- Scientists can ____ areas relatively ____ by people.
- knowledge allows ____ to be ____ in ____ managed → ____ preserved.
- they're extremely ____.

Damaged ⬃⬂ Species are

take a ____ → struggle to
time to regrow. adapt to change.

Conservation & Development

International Agreements:
1959 ____ — tourism ____ to protect fragile ____.
- Visitors ____ to ____.
- Peaceful ____ activities.
- ____ activity prohibited.
- Cruises with ____ can't stop.

Role of Governments:
Laws (e.g. 1964 ____) can prevent ____ in wilderness areas → reduced ____ over land.

Using Technology:
Modern ____ methods minimise ____ impacts → ____ beds stop ____ buildings melting permafrost.

Conservation Groups:
These ____ governments to ____ cold ____ → more ____ development.

 ☑ ☑ ☑

CASE STUDY # Alaska and Sustainable Management

Opportunities and Challenges in Alaska

Energy	Mineral resources	Fishing	Tourism
Oil	Gold	2016 —	2 million
Trans-	$154 million	and employed	and generate

Inaccessibility:
- Remote, mountainous

- Air
- Ice
- Some roads close

- Small, scattered
  → far from

Extreme Temperatures:
- Extreme cold is
- Daylight hours

Buildings and Infrastructure:
- Soft / frozen

- Construction only
- Pipelines built on

Barrow, gets 67 days of

Cold Environments — Value

WILDERNESS AREA —

They need to be _____ because:
- they provide

- scientists can

- knowledge allows

- they're extremely

Damaged plants   Species are

Conservation & Development

International Agreements:
1959 Antarctica Treaty

- Visitors
- Peaceful
- Nuclear activity
- Cruises with

Role of Governments:
Laws (e.g. 1964 Wilderness Act)

Using Technology:
Modern construction methods minimise
environmental damage →

Conservation Groups
These pressure governments to

Mixed Practice Quizzes

Time to get your crampons on and see if you have a firm grip in the icy material on p.43-46. Mark each of the four quizzes yourself and tot up your scores.

Quiz 1 Date: ...... / ...... / ......

1) Give two reasons why cold wilderness areas are extremely fragile.
2) How cold (in °C) can it be in polar areas?
3) Define 'wilderness area'.
4) Give two groups of people that inhabit tundra areas.
5) Why might global warming cause animals to migrate closer to the poles?
6) Explain why plant growth is limited in cold environments.
7) Describe the plant life in tundra environments.
8) Describe the kinds of plant roots you might find in a cold environment.
9) What does the Trans-Alaska pipeline connect?
10) Give an example of how technology can minimise impacts on cold environments.

Total:

Quiz 2 Date: ...... / ...... / ......

1) Why do animals in cold environments often hibernate?
2) How can governments conserve cold environments?
3) True or false? Biodiversity in cold environments is very low.
4) Why do carnivores in cold environments rarely stay in the same area year-round?
5) How cold (in °C) can it be in tundra areas?
6) How do birds in cold environments avoid the harshest conditions?
7) Give three minerals mined in Alaska.
8) Name two types of plants found in polar areas.
9) Why can getting around in Alaska be difficult in the summer?
10) What type of cold environment can reindeer be found in?

Total:

Mixed Practice Quizzes

Quiz 3   Date: ...... / ...... / ......

1) Why is construction expensive in Alaska?
2) Describe the soil in tundra environments.
3) Why does global warming put polar species at risk of decline or extinction?
4) How does melting permafrost affect the global environment?
5) Give three protective measures set out in the 1959 Antarctica Treaty.
6) Why do predators in cold environments have white winter coats?
7) Give two reasons why wilderness areas should be conserved.
8) What industries generate more than half of Alaska's income?
9) What might herbivores in cold environments do to find food when plant growth is limited?
10) Describe the climate of polar environments.

Total:

Quiz 4   Date: ...... / ...... / ......

1) Why are pipelines in Alaska built on stilts?
2) Name two animals typically found in polar areas.
3) Explain how conserving cold environments can lead to the preservation of rare species.
4) Describe the interdependence of plants and permafrost.
5) How does having small leaves benefit plants in cold environments?
6) Describe the seasons experienced by tundra environments.
7) Give three reasons why many parts of Alaska might be considered inaccessible.
8) Explain how people trampling plants could lead to other problems in cold environments.
9) How many people were employed by the Alaskan fishing industry in 2016?
10) How do conservation groups attempt to protect cold environments?

Total:

The UK Physical Landscape

First Go:
..... / ..... / .....

Upland and Lowland Areas in the UK

▓ _____ areas — formed of hard, _____ (e.g. _____) and _____ (e.g. _____ and _____) rocks that are resistant to _____ .

▒ _____ areas — formed of softer _____ rocks (e.g. _____ and _____) that _____ more easily.

> Most cities are in _____ and often _____ on the UK's _____ .

> _____ , the highest mountain in the UK, is in the _____ .

Spey

_____ Mountains in Scottish Highlands. _____ and _____ populated.

River Clyde Lower Valley — the Clyde has a _____ valley and _____ . _____ is on the flood plain.

Tay

Tweed

_____

Lake District — an _____ . _____ features, _____ .

Holderness Coast — mainly made of soft _____ . Cliffs eroding _____ .

_____ **Mountains**

Pennines

_____

Snowdonia — upland area with _____ and _____ , e.g. _____ .

> Snowdonia is formed from _____ from an _____ .

Wye

Great Ouse

_____

_____ — marshy, flat, _____ . A lot of the land has been _____ for _____ .

Dorset Coast — bands of _____ and _____ rock. Leads to landforms such as _____ and _____ .

The UK Physical Landscape

Upland and Lowland Areas in the UK

Upland areas — formed of

Lowland areas — formed of

Most cities are in .... and often ....

...................., the highest .... is in ....

Grampian Mountains

River Clyde Lower Valley —

Lake District —

Holderness Coast —

Pennines

Snowdonia —

Snowdonia is formed ....

The Fens —

Dorset Coast —

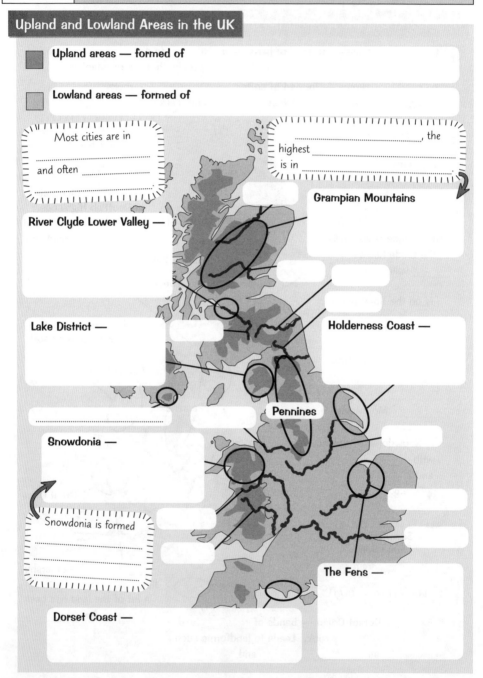

Coastal Processes

Weathering and Mass Movement

MECHANICAL WEATHERING — the breakdown of rock

_____ , e.g. _____ .

CHEMICAL WEATHERING — the breakdown of rock by

_____ , e.g. _____ .

MASS MOVEMENT — _____ acts on rock / loose material
→ material _____ .

Slides:	Slumps:	Rockfalls:
____ plane	____	____ plane

 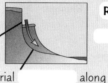

Material shifts in a _____ .

Material _____ along a _____ slip plane

Material _____ and falls _____ .

Destructive Waves

Destructive waves _____ the _____ .

_____ waves are _____ ,
_____ and _____

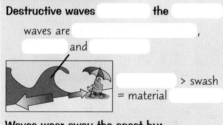

_____ > swash
= material _____

Waves wear away the coast by:

* _____ power (air forced into rock)
* _____ (scraping / rubbing of rock)
* _____ (rocks collide, break and smooth)

Constructive Waves

Constructive waves _____ material.

_____ waves are _____ ,
_____ and _____

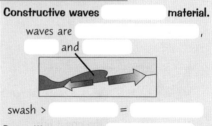

swash > _____ = _____

Deposition — waves _____
and _____ sediment when:

* rolling _____ beach and _____
* lots of material is _____
  _____ the area

Transportation — Longshore Drift

LONGSHORE DRIFT
— _____
movement of _____
_____

Waves follow _____ .

_____ carries material up the beach.

_____ carries material back down beach.

Water moves sediment by
....
and ....

Coastal Processes

Weathering and Mass Movement

MECHANICAL WEATHERING —

CHEMICAL WEATHERING —

MASS MOVEMENT —
→

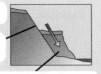

Slumps:

Destructive Waves

waves are

>
= material removed

Waves wear away the coast by:

-
-
-

Constructive Waves

waves are

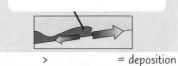

> = deposition

Deposition — waves lose energy and drop sediment when:
- rolling

- lots of

Transportation — Longshore Drift

LONGSHORE DRIFT
—

Swash

Backwash

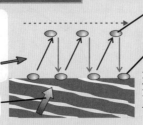

Coastal Landforms

Landforms Caused by Deposition

BEACHES — formed by

.

SPITS — formed when

transports   past

forms recurved end

area behind spit sheltered
— material accumulates,
        grow

BARS — formed when a

joins   .

forms

behind bar

bay

SAND DUNES — formed when

is

sand deposited   dune

forms

        dune

plants   and more   accumulates

Landforms Caused by Erosion

HEADLANDS and BAYS:

rock

erodes

to form

soft

hard

CAVES, ARCHES and STACKS:

over time

arch

enlarge   weakens   remains

— caves form   and collapses

WAVE-CUT PLATFORMS:

① Erosion
causes
....
....

② Rock
above
....

③ New
....
....

④ .... retreats.
wave-cut
platform.

Rock type affects landform development.
Coasts can be ....
or ....

HARD | SOFT

SOFT
HARD

Coastal Landscape — Dorset

EXAMPLE

Bands of   and   have eroded at   rates.

The Fleet

Chesil Beach —

Durdle Door —

Bournemouth

Weymouth

Old Harry —

The Foreland

Lulworth Cove —

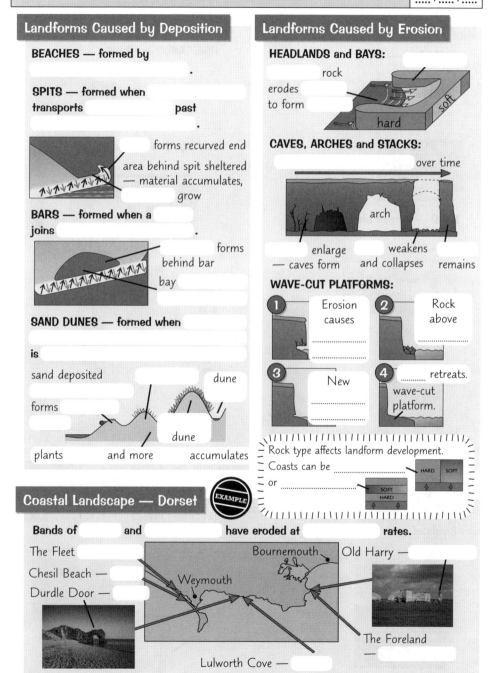

Coastal Landforms

Landforms Caused by Deposition

BEACHES —

SPITS — formed when

wind forms _____ end

area behind spit sheltered

BARS — formed when

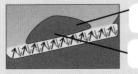

SAND DUNES — formed when

sand

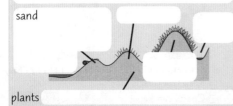

plants

Landforms Caused by Erosion

HEADLANDS and BAYS:

soft

hard

CAVES, ARCHES and STACKS:

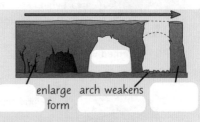

enlarge   arch weakens

form

WAVE-CUT PLATFORMS:

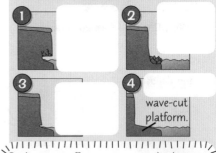

1   2

3   4

wave-cut platform.

Rock .... affects .... development.

Coasts can be ....

or ....

HARD   SOFT

SOFT
HARD

Coastal Landscape — Dorset

EXAMPLE

Bands of

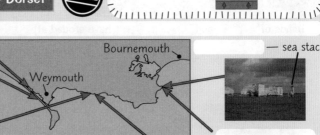

Lagoon

— bar

— arch

Weymouth

Bournemouth

— sea stack

— bay

Coastal Management

Management Strategies

Hard engineering — relatively .... but can be .... and need ....

1 **HARD ENGINEERING —** .... structures built to .... the .... of the ....

.... waves

absorbs wave ....

.... — reduces ....

longshore drift

.... material

2 **SOFT ENGINEERING —** uses knowledge of the .... and its ....

beach .... and ....

.... — waves

added material

dune ....

.... plants .... dunes — dunes form

.... dunes

.... in ....

Soft engineering — more .... but can be ....

3 **MANAGED RETREAT —** .... removing .... and ....

land becomes .... — protects land behind from .... and ....

Managed retreat is .... and .... but may ....

UK Coastal Management — Lyme Regis

EXAMPLE

Powerful waves .... the .... around Lyme Regis, in SW England.
Properties have been damaged by .... and ....

LYME REGIS
Drainage work
Sea wall
Rock armour
Replenished beach
Rock armour

Phase
■ I
▨ II
☐ III (not done)
▨ IV

Rock armour

1990s-2015 — .... phases of ....
.... and .... engineering strategies used to .... town from ....

Benefits:
• .... trade in some parts of town
• .... and .... protected
• easier to ....

Conflicts:
• more tourists = ...
• harder to find and excavate ....
• very ...., may need rebuilding.

Coastal management needed because:
• 3600+ .... in Lyme Regis.
• Local economy depends on ....
• .... would have been lost.

Coastal Management

Management Strategies

Hard engineering — _____ but _____ replacing.

1 **HARD ENGINEERING** — man-made structures

longshore drift

absorbs

traps

2 **SOFT ENGINEERING** —

beach and

added material

dune

plants

Soft engineering — ....

3 **MANAGED RETREAT** —

land becomes

Managed retreat is .... but

UK Coastal Management — Lyme Regis

EXAMPLE

Powerful waves erode
Properties

Drainage work

LYME REGIS

Sea wall
Rock armour

Replenished beach

Rock armour

Phase
■ I
▨ II
☐ III (not done)
▨ IV

Rock armour

1990s-2015 — Four phases

Benefits:
• ....
• ....
• ....

Conflicts:
• ....
• harder to find ....
• very expensive, ...

Coastal management needed because:
•
•

• **900 m of road**

Mixed Practice Quizzes

Test what you've covered on p.49-56 by tackling these four quizzes. If you're scoring high, then keep up the work and you'll coast your way through the exam...

Quiz 1

Date: ...... / ...... / ......

1) Name one type of mechanical weathering.
2) Give three ways that waves can erode the coast.
3) What is the difference between discordant and concordant coastlines?
4) What types of rock are upland areas usually formed from?
5) Give the name of a famous sea stack.
6) Which type of wave deposits material on coastlines?
7) Give an example of chemical weathering.
8) Name four coastal landforms caused by deposition.
9) What is the name for the curved tip of a spit formed by the wind?
10) What type of management strategy is rock armour?

Total:

Quiz 2

Date: ...... / ...... / ......

1) Name two soft engineering strategies used to protect the coast from erosion.
2) True or false? Constructive waves erode the coast.
3) Which man-made structure traps material moved by longshore drift?
4) What is mechanical weathering?
5) Explain how longshore drift happens.
6) How is a bar formed?
7) Are sedimentary rocks more likely to be found in upland or lowland areas?
8) Which coastal landform do wave-cut notches develop into over time?
9) Give three reasons why the hard engineering strategies used to protect Lyme Regis were needed.
10) Describe how a crack in a headland could eventually develop into a sea stack.

Total:

Mixed Practice Quizzes

Quiz 3   Date: ...... / ...... / ......

1) How does a wave-cut platform form? ☑
2) What process involves material shifting in a straight line down a slope? ☑
3) How does a gabion protect the coast from erosion? ☑
4) Name five rivers in the UK. ☑
5) Describe the characteristics of destructive waves. ☑
6) Give two management strategies that have been used to prevent erosion around Lyme Regis. ☑
7) What is the aim of a hard engineering strategy? ☑
8) True or false? The Lake District is a lowland area. ☑
9) Name three coastal landforms caused by erosion. ☑
10) If a wave's backwash is more powerful than its swash, will material be removed or deposited? ☑

Total:

Quiz 4   Date: ...... / ...... / ......

1) Give the name of a famous arch on the UK's coastline. ☑
2) Describe the characteristics of constructive waves. ☑
3) Describe how a spit forms. ☑
4) What is managed retreat and how does it work? ☑
5) What type of waves form beaches? ☑
6) What is chemical weathering? ☑
7) How does dune regeneration reduce flooding? ☑
8) Name three types of sand dune. ☑
9) Name the two types of coastline that are formed by alternating bands of hard and soft rock (that are parallel to, or at right angles to the coast). ☑
10) Describe what happens in a 'slump'. ☑

Total:

The River Valley and Fluvial Processes

River Profiles

LONG PROFILE — shows .... along river course.

CROSS PROFILE — shows what .... looks like.

upland area

source

....

...... or ......

Cross profile determined
by type of .... :

course	gradient	valley and channel shape	cross profile
upper	....	.... valley, ... sides. .... channel.	
middle	....	.... valley sides. .... channel.	
lower	....	.... valley. .... channel.	

Vertical erosion — .... river valley and
channel, making it ....
Dominant in ....

Lateral erosion — .... river valley and
channel. Dominant in
....

Processes of Erosion

- **HYDRAULIC ACTION —**
  force of ....
  .... the river channel.

- **ABRASION —**
  eroded rocks ....
  .... river channel.

- **ATTRITION —**
  Eroded rocks .... /
  .... and smooth edges.

- **SOLUTION —** ....
  some rocks .... , e.g. ....

Transportation of Eroded Material

TRACTION — .... particles
.... along the river bed.

SALTATION —
.... particles are
.... the river bed.

SUSPENSION — ....
particles are carried along.

SOLUTION — materials
.... in the water
and are carried along.

Deposition

DEPOSITION — when a river ....

Occurs when rivers lose .... and .... Rivers slow because:

- The water is ....
- The river reaches its ....
- The volume of water ....
- The amount of .... material ....

Smaller particles → transported .... → deposited ....

Deposition is
dominant in the
.... course.

The River Valley and Fluvial Processes

Second Go:
..... / ..... / .....

River Profiles

LONG PROFILE —

CROSS PROFILE —

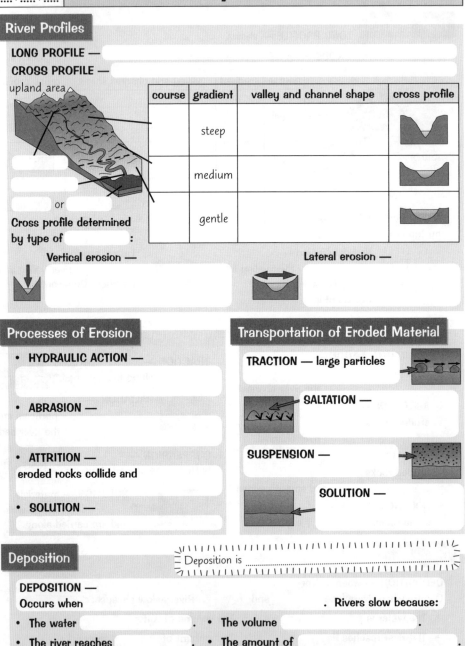

upland area

or

**Cross profile determined
by type of** :

course	gradient	valley and channel shape	cross profile
	steep		
	medium		
	gentle		

Vertical erosion —

Lateral erosion —

Processes of Erosion

- **HYDRAULIC ACTION —**

- **ABRASION —**

- **ATTRITION —**
eroded rocks collide and

- **SOLUTION —**

Transportation of Eroded Material

TRACTION — large particles

SALTATION —

SUSPENSION —

SOLUTION —

Deposition

Deposition is ....

DEPOSITION —
Occurs when . **Rivers slow because:**

- The water . • The volume .

- The river reaches . • The amount of .

Smaller → → deposited closer .

River Landforms

Landforms Resulting from Erosion

WATERFALLS and GORGES

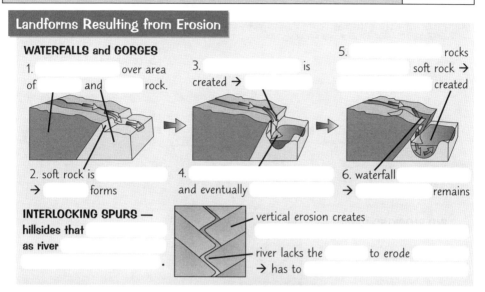

1. [_____] over area of [____] and [____] rock.

2. soft rock is [_____] → [_____] forms

3. [_____] is created → [_____]

4. [_____] and eventually [_____]

5. [_____] rocks soft rock → [_____] created

6. waterfall → [_____] remains

INTERLOCKING SPURS — hillsides that [_____] as river [_____].

vertical erosion creates [_____]

river lacks the [____] to erode → has to [_____]

Landforms Resulting from Erosion and Deposition

MEANDERS — [_____] in a river's [_____].

Thalweg — line of .... and ....

aerial view:

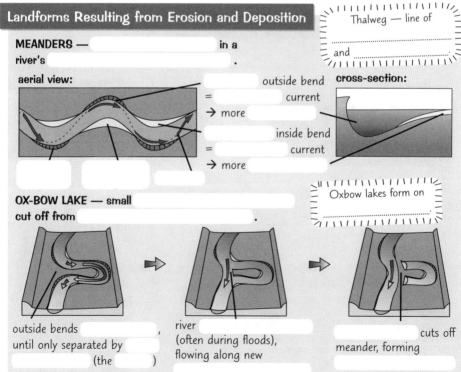

[_____] outside bend = [_____] current → more [_____]

[_____] inside bend = [_____] current → more [_____]

cross-section:

OX-BOW LAKE — small [_____] cut off from [_____].

Oxbow lakes form on ....

outside bends [_____], until only separated by [____] (the [____])

river [_____] (often during floods), flowing along new [_____]

[_____] cuts off meander, forming [_____]

River Landforms

Landforms Resulting from Erosion

_____ and _____

1. river

3. steep

5. collapsed

2. soft

4. hard

6. waterfall

INTERLOCKING SPURS —

vertical

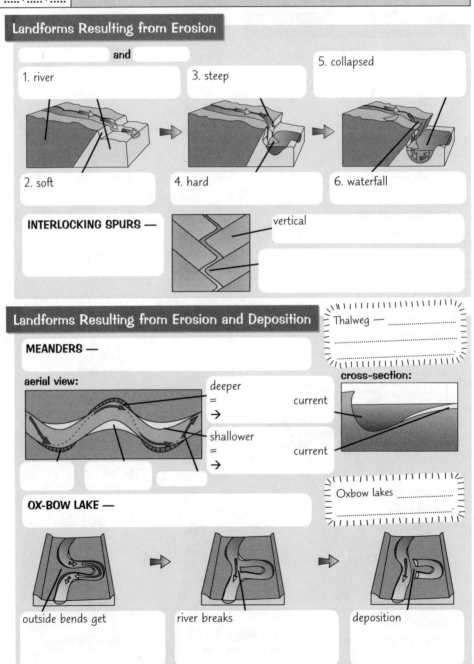

Landforms Resulting from Erosion and Deposition

Thalweg — ....

MEANDERS —

aerial view:

deeper
=   current
→

shallower
=   current
→

cross-section:

Oxbow lakes ....

OX-BOW LAKE —

outside bends get

river breaks

deposition

River Landforms

Landforms Resulting from Deposition

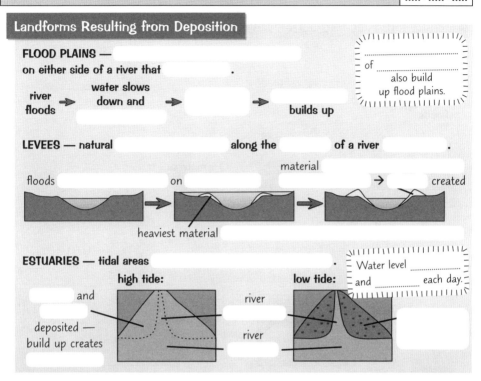

FLOOD PLAINS — _____
on either side of a river that _____ .

river floods → water slows down and _____ → _____ → builds up

_____ of _____ also build up flood plains.

LEVEES — natural _____ along the _____ of a river _____ .

floods _____ on _____ material _____ → _____ created

heaviest material _____

ESTUARIES — tidal areas _____ .

Water level _____ and _____ each day.

high tide: _____ and _____ deposited — build up creates _____ river

low tide: river _____ _____

The River Clyde

EXAMPLE

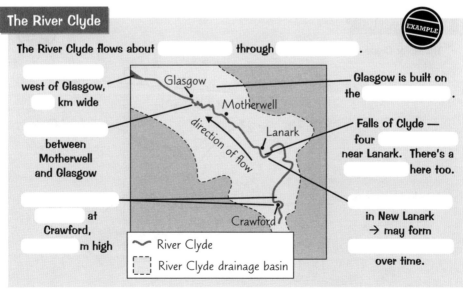

The River Clyde flows about _____ through _____ .

west of Glasgow, _____ km wide

_____ between Motherwell and Glasgow

Glasgow

Motherwell

direction of flow

Lanark

_____ at Crawford, _____ m high

Crawford

~ River Clyde
⬚ River Clyde drainage basin

Glasgow is built on the _____ .

Falls of Clyde — four _____ near Lanark. There's a _____ here too.

_____ in New Lanark → may form _____ over time.

 ✓ ✓ ✓

River Landforms

Landforms Resulting from Deposition

FLOOD PLAINS —

Slip-off ....
....
....
....

river
floods → ⬜ → ⬜ → ⬜

LEVEES —

floods deposit ⬜ material

ESTUARIES —

tide: tide:

Water ....
....

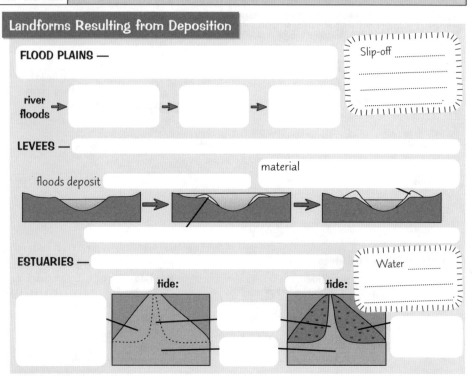

The River Clyde

EXAMPLE

The River Clyde _____.

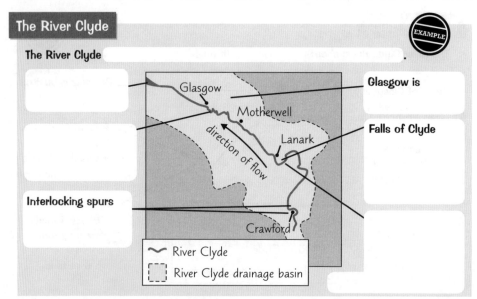

Glasgow

Motherwell

direction of flow

Lanark

Glasgow is

Falls of Clyde

Interlocking spurs

Crawford

~ River Clyde

⌐¬ River Clyde drainage basin

Mixed Practice Quizzes

Keep your knowledge flowing by testing what you've learnt from p.59-64.
Try out these four quizzes and go back and learn anything you're struggling with.

Quiz 1   Date: ...... / ...... / ......

1) In which two courses of a river is lateral erosion dominant?
2) Explain how an ox-bow lake forms.
3) Which course of a river tends to have the steepest gradient?
4) Explain how a flood plain builds up.
5) Describe the shape of a river's channel in its upper course.
6) What landform can be seen on the River Clyde at Crawford?
7) What does a river's 'long profile' show?
8) Explain how a waterfall forms.
9) Name the four processes of erosion that happen in a river.
10) Name the process of transportation that pushes large rocks along a riverbed.

Total:

Quiz 2   Date: ...... / ...... / ......

1) True or false? Rivers transport large particles further than small particles.
2) What is a river's 'thalweg'?
3) Describe the valley shape in the middle course of a river.
4) Explain how a waterfall can create a gorge.
5) What is a tidal area where a river meets the sea called?
6) What is deposition?
7) Which country does the River Clyde flow through?
8) What is a levee?
9) Which profile of a river shows what its cross-section looks like?
10) What type of erosion is dominant in a river's upper course?

Total:

Mixed Practice Quizzes

Quiz 3 Date: ...... / ...... / ......

1) What's the name for a natural embankment along the edge of a river channel?

2) What happens during attrition?

3) Which profile of a river shows how the gradient changes along its course?

4) Is a river channel's current faster on the inside of a bend or on the outside of a bend?

5) In which course does a river tend to have a very wide, deep channel?

6) What river landform is Glasgow built on?

7) True or false? The lower course of a river tends to have the steepest gradient.

8) What are mudflats built up from?

9) What type of river landform can form on a meander?

10) Name the four processes of transportation that happen in a river.

Total:

Quiz 4 Date: ...... / ...... / ......

1) What are interlocking spurs? Why do they form?

2) Which course of a river tends to have a V-shaped valley with steep sides?

3) Explain how:
   a) river cliffs form,
   b) slip-off slopes form.

4) True or false? Abrasion is when eroded rocks collide and break up.

5) What is a meander?

6) What is a flood plain?

7) What does the cross profile of a river show?

8) True or false? Levees form due to deposition.

9) Give two reasons why a river might slow down.

10) What is 'saltation'?

Total:

Flooding and Flood Management

Hydrographs

RIVER DISCHARGE — ⬚ flowing per ⬚.
Measured in ⬚ (⬚ m³/s).

HYDROGRAPH — a graph that shows how ⬚ changes over time in relation to ⬚.

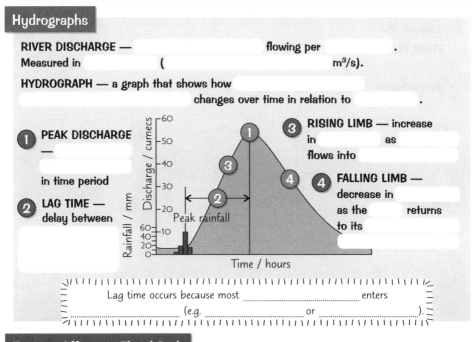

1 PEAK DISCHARGE — ⬚ ⬚ in time period

2 LAG TIME — delay between ⬚

3 RISING LIMB — increase in ⬚ as ⬚ flows into ⬚

4 FALLING LIMB — decrease in ⬚ as the ⬚ returns to its ⬚

Lag time occurs because most ⬚ enters ⬚ (e.g. ⬚ or ⬚).

Factors Affecting Flood Risk

PHYSICAL FACTORS

Relief
- Steeper ⬚ → water flows into ⬚ → discharge ⬚

Geology
- ⬚ soils and some ⬚ are ⬚, increasing ⬚.

Heavy rainfall
- Water arrives too ⬚ to infiltrate. Lots of surface runoff ⬚.

AND/ OR

Prolonged rainfall
- Saturates the ⬚ so further rainfall can't ⬚, increasing ⬚ into ⬚.

HUMAN FACTORS

Remember, ⬚ peak discharge = ⬚ flood risk

Land use
- Impermeable ⬚ (e.g. ⬚) increase ⬚. Drains ⬚ transport runoff to rivers, ⬚.

- Trees ⬚ and ⬚ rainwater → cutting them down ⬚ the amount of water ⬚.

Flooding and Flood Management

Hydrographs

RIVER DISCHARGE —

HYDROGRAPH — a graph that shows

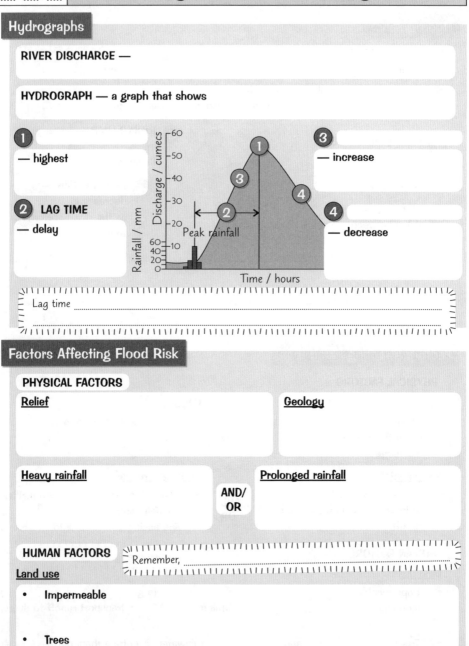

1
— highest

3
— increase

2 LAG TIME
— delay

4
— decrease

Peak rainfall

Lag time ....

Factors Affecting Flood Risk

PHYSICAL FACTORS

Relief

Geology

Heavy rainfall

Prolonged rainfall

AND/OR

HUMAN FACTORS

Remember, ...

Land use

• Impermeable

• Trees

Flooding and Flood Management

Management Strategies for Flooding

HARD ENGINEERING — ....
built to .... of rivers
and ....

Method	Benefits	Disadvantages
Dams and reservoirs	Control .... Potential for	Dams are .... Construction can ....
Channel straightening	Water leaves area → less	Flooding may happen .... Fast-moving water causes ....
Embankments	River capacity	Expensive. Can ....
Flood relief channels	Control over	Increased .... where .... rejoins the river.

SOFT ENGINEERING — .... set up using ....
and its ....

Method	Benefits	Disadvantages
Flood warnings & preparation	Give people time to .... /	Not .... Building modification is .... False ....
Flood plain zoning	Fewer .... surfaces reduces flood .... and	Urban .... limited. Can't help .... settlements.
Planting trees	Less .... and .... erosion.	Less ....
River restoration	Lower .... Requires little .... Better	Local flood risk can ....

Flood Management Scheme — Oxford

2007 floods → .... evacuated.

EXAMPLE

Scheme will protect ...., divert water from .... areas and involve:

• increased .... • bypass .... • .... trees • flood ....

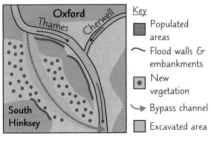

Key
- ▨ Populated areas
- ⌒ Flood walls & embankments
- ◉ New vegetation
- ↘ Bypass channel
- ▨ Excavated area

	Issues	Benefits
Social	Forced land .... construction.	Footpaths .... Residents feel ....
Econ.	Expensive (.............).	.... buildings protected. Cheaper ....
Envir.	.... trees felled.	New riverside ....

 ☑ ☑   ☑

Flooding and Flood Management

Management Strategies for Flooding

HARD ENGINEERING — ....
....

Method	Benefits	Disadvantages
Dams and reservoirs	Control	Dams are
straightening	Water →	Flooding Fast moving water
Embankments	River	Expensive.
Flood relief	Control	Increased

SOFT ENGINEERING — ....
....

Method	Benefits	Disadvantages
Flood warnings & preparation	Give people	Not . Building False
Flood plain	Fewer	Urban Can't help
Planting trees	Less	Less
River restoration	Lower	Local

Flood Management Scheme — Oxford

.... → EXAMPLE

Scheme will

• increased   •   •   •

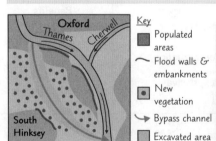

Key
- Populated areas
- Flood walls & embankments
- New vegetation
- Bypass channel
- Excavated area

	Issues	Benefits
Social	Forced	Footpaths
Econ.		
Envir.		New

Mixed Practice Quizzes

Now that you have been flooded with information from p.67-70, stop and test yourself by working through these quizzes. It's a great way to see what you know.

Quiz 1 Date: ...... / ...... / ......

1) True or false? Steeper valley sides cause a slow increase in river discharge during rainfall.
2) How do hard engineering structures tackle flooding?
3) Give two soft engineering flood management strategies.
4) What does a hydrograph show?
5) Give two benefits of building dams and reservoirs.
6) Now give two disadvantages of building dams and reservoirs.
7) Give one environmental issue and one environmental benefit caused by the flood management scheme in Oxford.
8) How does building embankments reduce flooding?
9) Give one disadvantage of reducing flooding by planting trees.
10) What does the rising limb on a hydrograph show?

Total:

Quiz 2 Date: ...... / ...... / ......

1) Give two ways that human land use can affect flood risk.
2) Describe the benefits and disadvantages of flood plain zoning.
3) On a hydrograph, what does the peak discharge show?
4) How does channel straightening help to reduce flooding?
5) What was the aim of the flood management scheme in Oxford?
6) What part of a hydrograph shows the increase in discharge as rain flows into the river?
7) What unit is river discharge measured in?
8) Give two features of the flood management scheme in Oxford.
9) What's the name for the delay between peak rainfall and peak discharge?
10) Give two economic benefits of the flood management scheme in Oxford.

Total:

Mixed Practice Quizzes

Quiz 3   Date: ...... / ...... / ......

1) What is 'river discharge'?
2) True or false? Clay soils are impermeable.
3) What is shown by the falling limb on a hydrograph?
4) What are 'soft engineering' flood management strategies?
5) Give two ways that rainfall can increase flood risk.
6) How many home were evacuated in the 2007 Oxford floods?
7) Give one advantage and one disadvantage of providing flood warnings.
8) Why does lag time occur?
9) Describe the benefits and disadvantages of flood relief channels.
10) True or false? Peak discharge is the highest point on a hydrograph.

Total:

Quiz 4   Date: ...... / ...... / ......

1) What is 'lag time' on a hydrograph?
2) Give two hard engineering flood management strategies.
3) Why does cutting down trees increase the amount of rainwater entering river channels?
4) What does 'cumecs' stand for?
5) How can the geology of an area affect flood risk?
6) Outline the disadvantages of channel straightening.
7) What part of a hydrograph shows the decrease in discharge as a river returns to its normal level?
8) Give two social issues linked to the flood management scheme in Oxford.
9) Explain how prolonged rainfall can increase flood risk.
10) How can human development in an area increase flood risk?

Total:

Glacial Processes

Erosion and Weathering

Glaciers move _____ due to the _____ of _____ .

BASAL SLIDING — the _____ of glaciers
using _____ under _____ as _____ .

Glaciers _____ in two ways:

ABRASION — _____ stuck in the ice _____ rock _____ the glacier.

PLUCKING — _____ at base / back / sides of glacier freezes onto rock.
Glacier moves _____ → pieces of _____ .

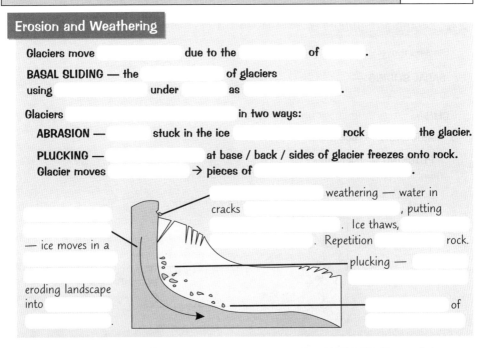

_____ weathering — water in _____ cracks _____ , putting _____ . Ice thaws, _____ . Repetition _____ rock.

_____ — ice moves in a _____

_____ plucking — _____

eroding landscape into _____

_____ of _____

Transportation & Deposition

TILL — mixture of _____ _____ .

Glaciers can _____ over large distances. Material can be:

• _____ into glacier

• carried _____

• _____ (bulldozing)

Material _____ valley floor when:

• the glacier is _____

• the _____

Fine material (e.g. _____)
washed away from front of _____
by _____ streams. Streams
sort material by _____ and deposit it in _____ .

Historical Ice Coverage — UK

Many glacial periods in last _____ m years.
Last glacial period about _____ yrs ago.
Ice has _____ .

Scotland

_____

Leeds

Ireland

Wales

Bristol Channel

Glacial Processes

Erosion and Weathering

Glaciers move _____ .

BASAL SLIDING — _____

Glaciers _____ :

   ABRASION — rock stuck

   PLUCKING — meltwater

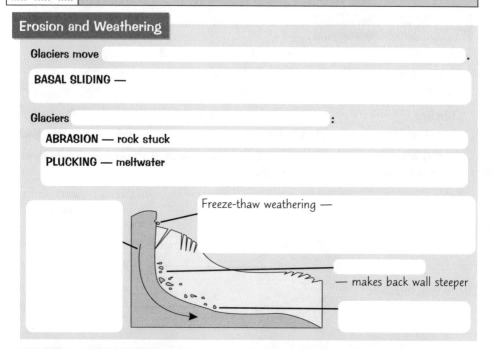

Freeze-thaw weathering —

— makes back wall steeper

Transportation & Deposition

TILL —

Glaciers can _____
_____ . Material can be:

   •

   •

   •

Material deposited on valley floor when:

   •

   •

Fine material

Streams

Historical Ice Coverage — UK

Many

Glacial Landforms

Landforms of Glacial Erosion

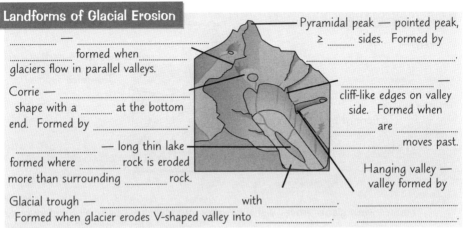

.... — .... formed when glaciers flow in parallel valleys.

Corrie — .... shape with a .... at the bottom end. Formed by ....

.... — long thin lake formed where .... rock is eroded more than surrounding .... rock.

Glacial trough — .... with .... Formed when glacier erodes V-shaped valley into ....

Pyramidal peak — pointed peak, ≥ .... sides. Formed by ....

.... — cliff-like edges on valley side. Formed when .... are .... moves past.

Hanging valley — valley formed by ....

Landforms of Glacial Deposition

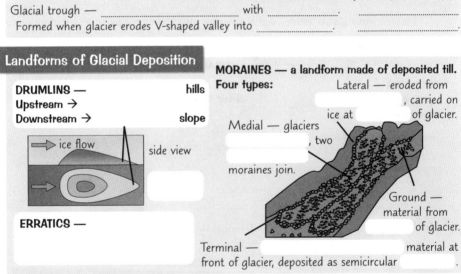

DRUMLINS — .... hills
Upstream → ....
Downstream → .... slope

ice flow   side view

ERRATICS —

MORAINES — a landform made of deposited till.
Four types:

Lateral — eroded from ...., carried on ice at .... of glacier.

Medial — glaciers ...., two .... moraines join.

Ground — material from .... of glacier.

Terminal — .... material at front of glacier, deposited as semicircular ....

Glacial Landforms — Snowdonia

EXAMPLE

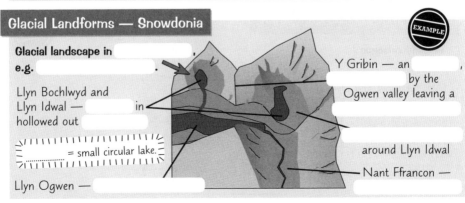

Glacial landscape in .... , **e.g.** ....

Llyn Bochlwyd and Llyn Idwal — .... in hollowed out ....

⌇⌇⌇⌇⌇ .... = small circular lake. ⌇⌇⌇⌇⌇

Llyn Ogwen — ....

Y Gribin — an ...., ... by the Ogwen valley leaving a ....

.... around Llyn Idwal

Nant Ffrancon — ....

Second Go:
..... / ..... / .....

Glacial Landforms

Landforms of Glacial Erosion

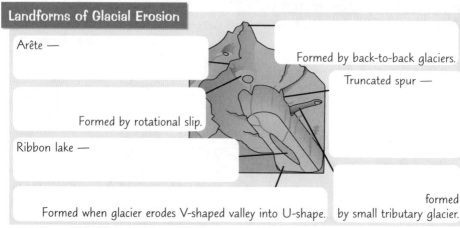

Arête —

Formed by back-to-back glaciers.

Truncated spur —

Formed by rotational slip.

Ribbon lake —

Formed when glacier erodes V-shaped valley into U-shape.

formed by small tributary glacier.

Landforms of Glacial Deposition

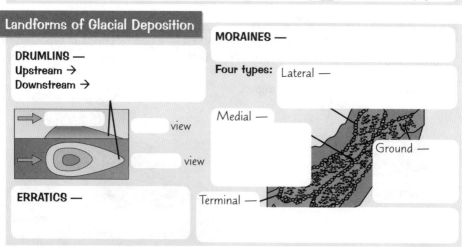

DRUMLINS —
Upstream →
Downstream →

MORAINES —

Four types: Lateral —

_____ view

Medial —

_____ view

Ground —

ERRATICS —

Terminal —

Glacial Landforms — Snowdonia

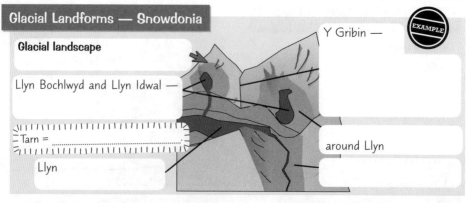

Glacial landscape

Y Gribin —

EXAMPLE

Llyn Bochlwyd and Llyn Idwal —

Tarn = ...

around Llyn

Llyn

Land Use in Glacial Landscapes

Economic Uses of Glaciated Areas

- Forestry — _____ grown
  in upland areas, used for _____
  _____ and _____ .

- Quarrying — for _____ ,
  _____ and _____ .

- Tourism — _____ and
  outdoor _____ attract tourists.

- Farming — _____ farming
  common in upland areas, _____
  _____ grown on valley floor.

> The people involved in these land uses can come
> _____ — tourists can
> _____ farming (e.g. _____) so
> farmers may _____

Development and Conservation — Conflicts

Developers think...	Conservationists think...
Tourism and farming provide _____ and contribute to the UK _____ .	Farming can _____ . Plantations don't support as many _____ as mixed forests.
Glacial areas can provide _____ (e.g. _____).	Developments and construction sites _____ and _____ . Logging _____ .
Developing _____ / _____ for tourists can _____ too.	Tourist infrastructure may be _____ — people _____ for their _____ .

Tourism — The Lake District

EXAMPLE

The Lake District National Park attracts almost _____ m tourists every year →
lots of _____ sites and outdoor _____ . Tourism has big impacts:

- Environmental — _____ erosion, cars _____ ,
  _____ on lakes.
- Economic — _____ supported, but work often _____ / _____ .
  Avg. house price _____ →
- Social — _____ , businesses _____ → everyday goods
  are _____ , ~25% of properties are _____ →
  there's limited / underfunded _____ for locals (e.g. _____ , schools, _____).

Strategies have been put in place to _____ :

- Traffic / parking — using _____ encouraged, improved _____
- Footpath erosion — resurfacing, _____ , _____ , _____
- Littering — _____ , _____ , volunteer _____
- Water / noise pollution — _____ , limited _____
- House prices — _____ , _____

 ☑   ☑ ☺ ☑

Unit 1C — Physical Landscapes in the UK

Land Use in Glacial Landscapes

Economic Uses of Glaciated Areas

- Forestry — coniferous forests

- Quarrying —

- Tourism —

- Farming —

The people involved in these land uses can come into conflict — ....
....
....
....
....

Development and Conservation — Conflicts

Developers think...	Conservationists think...
Tourism and farming	Farming can
Glacial areas	Developments and construction sites
Developing	Tourist infrastructure

Tourism — The Lake District

The Lake District National Park

- Environmental —

- Economic —

- Social —

Strategies have been put in place to tackle impacts of tourism:
- Traffic / parking — using
- Footpath erosion —
- Littering —
- Water / noise pollution —
- House prices —

Mixed Practice Quizzes

If it feels like your brain is moving at a glacial pace since completing p.73-78, get things up to speed again by having a go at these four mixed practice quizzes.

Quiz 1   Date: ...... / ...... / ....

1) What is a corrie?
2) What type of valley is formed from a small tributary glacier?
3) Name the four types of moraine.
4) What causes glaciers to move downhill?
5) Give two economic uses of glaciated areas.
6) Give one pro and one con of development in glacial landscapes.
7) What is 'abrasion' in a glacier?
8) How does an arête form?
9) Name the process in which ice moves in a circular motion, eroding the landscape into a bowl shape.
10) Give three strategies that have been put in place to tackle the impact of tourism in the Lake District National Park.

Total:

Quiz 2   Date: ...... / ...... / ....

1) What's the name for the mixture of material carried by glaciers?
2) How is medial moraine formed?
3) Name the two processes by which glaciers erode the landscape.
4) What is a glacial trough? How do they form?
5) Outline the economic impacts of tourism in the Lake District.
6) Give two reasons why a glacier might deposit material.
7) What type of farming is more likely:
   a) in an upland area?
   b) on a valley floor?
8) What is rotational slip?
9) Why is tourism popular in glaciated areas?
10) What is a truncated spur?

Total:

Mixed Practice Quizzes

Date: ...... / ...... / ......

1) Outline the social impacts of tourism in the Lake District.
2) What is moraine made from?
3) What is 'plucking'?
4) What is the name for a cliff-like edge on a valley side, formed when a ridge is cut off as a glacier moves past?
5) Give three ways that glaciers can transport material.
6) What is a drumlin? Describe its shape.
7) What's the name for a narrow, steep-sided ridge formed when two glaciers flow in parallel valleys?
8) What is basal sliding?
9) What is terminal moraine?
10) What is a tarn?

Total:

Quiz 4 Date: ...... / ...... / ......

1) What is outwash?
2) Which glacial landform is 'a pointed peak with more than three sides'?
3) What is the name for the movement of glaciers using meltwater under the ice as a lubricant?
4) Outline the environmental impacts of tourism in the Lake District.
5) What is an erratic?
6) Give two reasons why people might support conservation in glaciated areas.
7) Explain the process of freeze-thaw weathering.
8) Give one example of how land use in glacial areas might lead to conflict.
9) Which type of moraine is found at the front of a glacier?
10) When was the last glacial period?

Total:

Urban Growth

Urbanisation is Happening Fastest in Poorer Countries

URBANISATION — growth in proportion of people

	Urbanisation Rate	Approx. % in urban areas
	, less than 1%	
LICs	High, up to	30%
NEEs		

~55% world population lives in

Urbanisation has in HICs.

Causes of Urbanisation

RURAL-URBAN MIGRATION — movement from to .

Push Factors (from rural areas)	Pull Factors (to urban areas)
recovery from natural disasters.	jobs and pay.
Mechanisation → .	healthcare / education.
Desertification → land .	Family
Unstable income (dependent).	for better of life.

Young for work → have .

Better urban → life expectancy .

leads to

birth rate death rate = population .

INCREASE —

urbanisation rates → **MEGACITIES** — urban area with residents.

E.g. , India.

Lagos, Nigeria (an NEE) — Rapid Urban Growth

CASE STUDY

Regionally Important:
Migrant population = .

Well connected → important for .

Nationally Important:
% of Nigeria's industry.
until 1991.

Internationally Important:
West African centre.
5th largest African .
/ → global trade.

Population over .
Fast annual growth rate of because:
Independence from Colonial Rule in 1960:
— resources
(e.g. oil) no longer .
Gov. financed → jobs.

Natural Increase: rate > rate.
Rural-Urban Migration:
Escape .
Flee in neighbouring countries.

Nigeria's birthrate = people. World average .

& descendants returned from on.

Urban Growth

Urbanisation is Happening Fastest in Poorer Countries

URBANISATION —

	Urbanisation Rate	Approx. % in urban areas
HICs	Low,	
LICs		
NEEs	Around	

~ .... world population
lives in ....

Urbanisation ....
.... in HICs.

Causes of Urbanisation

RURAL-URBAN
MIGRATION —

Push Factors (from rural areas)	Pull Factors (to urban areas)
Slower recovery from	More jobs
→ fewer	Better
→ land	Family
Unstable income	Hope for better

Young →

Better →

leads to NATURAL INCREASE —
birth rates >
= population

High → MEGACITIES — urban area
with

E.g. ....

Lagos, Nigeria (an NEE) — Rapid Urban Growth

CASE STUDY

<u>Regionally Important:</u>
Migrant

Well
important

<u>Nationally Important:</u>
of
Capital

<u>Internationally Important:</u>
West African
largest
Port / airport →

Population
because:

<u>Independence from Colonial Rule in 1960:</u>
Economic
(e.g. oil)
Gov.

<u>Natural Increase:</u> Birth rate >

<u>Rural-Urban Migration:</u>
Escape
Flee
neighbouring

.... birthrate =
....
....
average = ...

.... & descendants returned from .... on.

Urban Growth — Lagos

 CASE STUDY

First Go:
..... / ..... / .....

Urban Growth in Lagos Compared to Rural Nigeria

SOCIAL:
- More _____ and _____ .
- Almost _____ schools.
- Better _____ to _____ .
- _____ water.

ECONOMIC:
- Incomes _____ .
- Lots of _____ .
- Government depts, manufacturing, _____ .
- Music and ' _____ ' film industry.

Five Challenges of Rapid Growth

.... of people in Lagos

1. **SLUMS & SQUATTER SETTLEMENTS:**
   - Housing _____ > supply → house prices _____ → _____ settlements (slums).
   - Housing = _____ → _____ to clean up city → evictions.

2. **LITTLE ACCESS TO CLEAN WATER, SANITATION AND ENERGY:**
   - Water demand > _____ → prices _____ by _____ .
   - _____ contaminates water sources → _____ , e.g. _____ .
   - Neighbourhoods take _____ to receive electricity. Some _____ connections.

3. **INSUFFICIENT SERVICES:**
   Many families can't afford _____ / _____ . Not enough facilities.

4. **UNEMPLOYMENT & CRIME:**
   _____ formal jobs → alternatives, e.g. scavenging / _____ .

   Informal jobs have no .... protection → stalls may be .... for .... developments.

5. **ENVIRONMENTAL ISSUES:**
   - Only _____ of waste collected. Dumps contain _____ .
   - _____ factory waste disposal → _____ .
   - Severe _____ → air pollution.

Urban Planning to Improve Quality of Life — Makoko

EXAMPLE

The _____ prototype was built in _____ :

SOCIAL BENEFITS
- _____ education.
- Built by locals — _____ .
- _____ spirit.

ECONOMIC BENEFITS
- Improved _____ .
- School success → gov. launch plan to _____ slum with _____ and biogas plant.

ENVIRONMENTAL BENEFITS
- _____ — used local materials, _____ and rainwater.
- Floats — _____ .

 ☑ ☑ ☑

CASE STUDY

Urban Growth — Lagos

Urban Growth in Lagos Compared to Rural Nigeria

SOCIAL:
- More hospitals and
- Almost
- Better access to
- Safe,

ECONOMIC:
- _____ up to
- Lots of
- Government depts,
- Music

Five Challenges of Rapid Growth

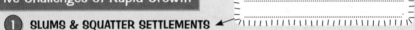

1 **SLUMS & SQUATTER SETTLEMENTS** ←

- Housing   → house prices rise →
- Housing = flimsy

2 **LITTLE ACCESS TO CLEAN WATER, SANITATION AND ENERGY**

- Water demand >
- Toilet waste contaminates
- Neighbourhoods take turns to receive

3 **INSUFFICIENT SERVICES**

Many families can't afford

4 **UNEMPLOYMENT & CRIME**

Too few

_____ have
_____
protection →
_____ may be
_____
for _____
developments.

5 **ENVIRONMENTAL ISSUES**

- Only 40% of waste
- Unregulated factory
- Severe

Urban Planning to Improve Quality of Life — Makoko

EXAMPLE

The _____ prototype was built in _____ :

SOCIAL BENEFITS:
- _____ education
- Built by

•

ECONOMIC BENEFITS:
- Improved
- School

ENVIRONMENTAL BENEFITS:
- Sustainable —

- Floats —

UK Cities

UK Cities — Distribution

The UK population distribution is very ....

_____ areas — easy to _____ , _____ climate.

Coastal — for _____ and _____ .

Near mineral deposits (e.g. _____) — _____ development.

CONURBATIONS —
urban areas formed by
_____ .

Liverpool — a Port City in North West England

CASE STUDY

On the River _____ estuary → export of _____ / _____ .

Internationally significant — UNESCO _____ .
many foreign tourists → major contribution to _____ .

Nationally significant — _____ manufacturing companies
→ _____ .

It's also the World Capital City of ...., and a European Capital of ....

Migration has influenced _____ :

1 National Migration:
Late 1700s / Early 1800s: _____ migrants
→ industry / _____ / _____ .
_____ : Irish migrants due to _____ .

2 International Migration:
Port built in _____ .
Europe's first _____ .
UK's oldest _____ community.

Liverpudlians have an ethnic minority background.

Urban Change in Liverpool — Opportunities

CASE STUDY

Port and manufacturing centre ➡ _____ and creative industries centre

ENVIRONMENTAL

_____ :

Developing and preserving _____ .

E.g. _____
shopping and leisure complex
includes a _____ .

_____ / pedestrian routes:

Reduced _____ .

Some .... remains, e.g. .... manufacturing at Halewood, and .... (container port, opened ....).

SOCIAL AND ECONOMIC

Cultural _____ :

Diversity in _____ , _____ , etc.

_____ / entertainment:
E.g. Echo Arena sport / concert venue
— on _____
(disused land) at _____ .

Employment:
160 000 _____ / _____ jobs.
' _____ Triangle' area: old factories /
warehouses → _____ industries.

Integrated transport systems:
_____ operates city's _____ ,
_____ and _____
— easy to get around.

Second Go:
..... / ..... / .....

UK Cities

UK Cities — Distribution

The .... is very uneven.

Lowland areas —

Coastal —

Near mineral deposits (e.g. coal) —   development.

CONURBATIONS —

Liverpool — a Port City in North West England

It's also the ....
....
and a ....
....

On

Internationally significant —

Nationally significant —   companies → 50 000+ jobs.

Migration has

1. **National Migration**

Late 1700s /

1845: Irish migrants

2. **International Migration**

.... in 1715.

Europe's

UK's oldest

1 in 8 Liverpudlians have an .... background.

Urban Change in Liverpool — Opportunities

CASE STUDY

Port & manufacturing centre →

ENVIRONMENTAL

Urban greening:
Developing

E.g.

Cycle / pedestrian routes:
Reduced

SOCIAL AND ECONOMIC

Cultural mixing:

Recreation / entertainment:
E.g.

Employment:

Integrated transport systems:
Merseytravel

Some ....,
remains, e.g. ....
at ...., and Liverpool2
(................................., opened ....).

UK Cities

Urban Change in Liverpool — Challenges

ENVIRONMENTAL:

<u>Dereliction</u>
Wealthy left → _____
_____ and _____,
e.g. _____ .

<u>Using brownfield / greenfield sites</u>
Suburbs _____ → construction on
greenfield _____ → _____ destroyed.
Brownfield sites — better for environment
but _____ .

<u>Waste disposal</u>
Population grows → _____ ,
less _____ .

SOCIAL AND ECONOMIC:

<u>Urban deprivation</u>
_____ decline → inner city v. deprived.

<u>Housing inequality</u>
Regeneration
replacement housing _____ to many.

<u>Education and employment inequality</u>
→ _____ incomes,
_____ unemployment.

Anfield youth
unemployment = ... %
UK avg. = ...

<u>Unhealthy lifestyles</u>
Drinking, smoking and poor diets common in
deprived areas → _____ expectancies.

Urban Sprawl — Pressure on Rural-Urban Fringe

Liverpool _____ → Merseyside _____ created.

Effects on rural-urban fringe:
Housing on _____ land → open spaces / ecosystems lost.
Out-of-town _____ , e.g. Knowsley Business Park,
on _____ land → rural land lost, _____ , congestion.

_____ settlements formed → challenges:
House prices _____ — locals can't _____ to stay.
Businesses _____ — people aren't around much.
Pollution, congestion and _____ problems increase.

URBAN SPRAWL —
unplanned _____ of urban areas into _____ .

RURAL-URBAN FRINGE —
where _____ and rural land uses _____ .

COMMUTER SETTLEMENTS
— places where _____ residents work _____ .

The Anfield Project — Urban Regeneration

Anfield was v. deprived — _____ housing , high _____
_____ regeneration project:

REGENERATION —
redevelopment of urban _____ to improve _____ of life.

SOCIAL AND ECONOMIC FEATURES:
> _____ spent _____ derelict housing.
Sports and Community Centre refurbished,
new _____ and _____ .
New _____ planned — existing and
local businesses _____ to move in.

ENVIRONMENTAL FEATURES:
_____ scheme to create
tree-lined, wider _____
and a _____ -friendly area.
Stanley Park —
_____ replaced, _____ improved.

 ✓ ✓ ✓

Unit 2A — Urban Issues and Challenges

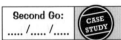

UK Cities

Urban Change in Liverpool — Challenges

ENVIRONMENTAL:

Dereliction:

Using brownfield / greenfield sites:

Brownfield sites — better for environment

Waste disposal:
Population

SOCIAL AND ECONOMIC:

Urban deprivation:

Housing inequality:
Regeneration

Education and employment inequality:

low
high

Unhealthy lifestyles:
Drinking

unemployment = ...
UK avg. =

Urban Sprawl — Pressure on Rural-Urban Fringe

Liverpool sprawled → Merseyside

Effects on rural-urban fringe:

Housing on greenfield land →

Out-of-town developments
on cheaper land →

Commuter settlements formed → challenges:

House prices rise —

Businesses suffer —

Pollution,

URBAN SPRAWL —

RURAL-URBAN FRINGE —

COMMUTER SETTLEMENTS —

The Anfield Project — Urban Regeneration

Anfield was v. deprived —

£

SOCIAL AND ECONOMIC FEATURES:

>£36m spent refurbishing

Sports and

New high street planned —
                      encouraged to move in.

REGENERATION —

ENVIRONMENTAL FEATURES:

£   scheme to

and a   -friendly area.

Stanley Park
                        improved.

Sustainable Urban Living

Water & Energy Conservation Schemes

WATER CONSERVATION

Take   as
is naturally   .
Schemes reduce usage by:
- collecting   for gardens
- efficient   • water

Curitiba, Brazil, cut water use with .... and having .... non-drinking water systems.

Curitiba also has .... for biodiesel buses.

ENERGY CONSERVATION

Burning fossil fuels is   :
- they'll   .
- they release   gases.

Use of fossil fuels reduced by:
- Promoting   — letting homeowners sell   from   panels.
- Efficiency rules for new   .
- Promoting public   use.

Green Space Creation

Green spaces...
- provide   away from bustle to relax in →   .
- encourage   /   →   benefits.
- reduce   pollution.
- reduce   → less   .

Curitiba landowners who created .... were ....

Waste Recycling

Landfill is   :
- space will   .
-      → greenhouse gases.
-      → saves   , less   .

Schemes include:
-      collections.
-      item recycling.
-      , e.g. Freecycle™.

In Curitiba, ... / .... are exchanged for recycling.

Traffic Congestion Causes Problems

environmental: /   .

economic: e.g.   .

social: e.g.   ,   , health issues.

Congestion can be   by:
     strategies which encourage public transport use, e.g.
- London Underground —   daily users.
- Electronic '   ' cards increase   of London transport.
- Self-service   in cities.

Managing   , e.g.
- Ring   and   areas.
-      charges.
-      — bus faster than driving.
- Parking   help traffic flow, e.g. '   '.

Sustainable Urban Living

Water & Energy Conservation Schemes

WATER CONSERVATION:

Schemes
- collecting
- efficient
- water

Curitiba, Brazil, cut water use with .... and having .... water systems.

*Curitiba also has ....
....
....
...................*

ENERGY CONSERVATION:

Burning

- they'll
- they release

Use of fossil fuels reduced by:
- Promoting

- Efficiency rules for
- Promoting   use.

Green Space Creation

Green spaces...

- provide

- encourage

- reduce

- reduce

*Curitiba landowners
....
....
...................*

Waste Recycling

Landfill
- space
- decomposition →

Recycling →

Schemes include:
-
- Large item
-

*In Curitiba,
....
....
....
are exchanged for recycling.*

Traffic Congestion Causes Problems

environmental:	economic: e.g.	social: e.g.

Congestion can be reduced by:

Urban transport strategies which encourage
                                    e.g.

- London

- Electronic 'Oyster Cards'

- Self-service

Managing traffic flow
-

-

- Bus lanes — bus   than driving.

- Parking restrictions

Mixed Practice Quizzes

Now I hope you've conserved your energy — we've (Liver)pooled the content from p.81-90 and sprawled it across four quizzes so you can check your progress.

Quiz 1   Date: ...... / ...... / ......

1) Give three factors that pull people to cities from rural areas.
2) Why are UK cities mostly located in lowland areas?
3) Give two reasons why Lagos is regionally important.
4) Give three socio-economic problems associated with deprivation in some inner-city areas of Liverpool.
5) Define the term 'urban sprawl'.
6) Why is the percentage of people living in urban areas much higher in HICs than in LICs and NEEs?
7) Give two reasons why Lagos is internationally important.
8) Give an example of urban greening in Liverpool.
9) Give two reasons why landfill is unsustainable.
10) Why might people who migrate to Lagos scavenge or join a gang to generate income?

Total:

Quiz 2   Date: ...... / ...... / ......

1) Give one reason why people migrate to Lagos from neighbouring countries.
2) Define the term 'urbanisation'.
3) Give an example of how a brownfield site has been used in Liverpool.
4) Give a problem associated with building on greenfield sites.
5) Give three social advantages of living in Lagos compared to rural Nigeria.
6) Give two reasons why burning fossil fuels is unsustainable.
7) Explain how the Merseyside conurbation formed.
8) How does agricultural mechanisation contribute to rural-urban migration?
9) Give three ways of managing traffic flow.
10) Name a problem associated with limited access to clean water in Lagos.

Total:

Mixed Practice Quizzes

Quiz 3   Date: ...... / ...... / ......

1) Why does rural-urban migration cause a natural increase in a city's population?

2) What is a 'conurbation'?

3) How did Lagos's independence from colonial rule boost its economic development?

4) State the two types of migration that influenced Liverpool's character.

5) Give one social, one economic and one environmental benefit of the Anfield project.

6) Give two ways that water consumption can be reduced.

7) Give three factors that push people from rural areas to cities.

8) Why are many cities established near coasts?

9) Give two problems that may affect a rural area that becomes a commuter settlement.

10) Give three economic advantages of living in Lagos compared to rural Nigeria.

Total:

Quiz 4   Date: ...... / ...... / ......

1) What is a 'megacity'? Give an example.

2) Why might a business choose to locate in an out-of-town development instead of in a city?

3) Suggest one reason why Liverpool developed on the River Mersey estuary.

4) Give two examples of recycling schemes that can reduce the amount of waste going to landfill.

5) Give three problems resulting from traffic congestion.

6) Give four problems caused by rapid population growth in Lagos.

7) Explain why Anfield urgently needed urban regeneration.

8) True or false? Liverpool is a European Capital of Culture.

9) Give an example of an urban planning scheme in Lagos.

10) Give an example of an urban transport strategy in London.

Total:

Measuring Development

First Go:
..... / ..... / .....

Measures of Development

DEVELOPMENT — a country's progress in _____ , use of _____ and improving _____ .

GLOBAL DEVELOPMENT — difference in _____ between _____ and developed countries.

Measure	What it is	= increases/decreases with development
Gross _____ Income (GNI) per _____ (in US$)	Total value of _____ and _____ produced in a _____ (inc. _____ income) by the _____ .	⬆
Birth rate	_____ births per _____ per _____ .	
_____	Deaths per _____ per _____ .	⬇
Infant _____ rate	No. of _____ who die before _____ , per _____ born.	
People _____ doctor	_____ no. people for each _____ .	⬇
Literacy rate	_____ adults who can _____ and _____ .	⬆
_____ to safe water	_____ with _____ water.	
Life _____	_____ lived to.	⬆

Limitations of measures:

- Variations _____ a country _____ shown.

- _____ indicators may be _____ .

> Qatar's GNI per person is high — _____ extremely rich but _____ poor.

> Cuba has low _____ but fairly high _____

Classification by Wealth

HIGHER _____ COUNTRIES
(_____)
— Wealthiest, _____ GNI per head.
E.g. UK, _____ , Canada, _____ .

_____ COUNTRIES (LICs)
— _____ , very _____ GNI per head.
E.g. Somalia and _____ .

> BRICS = Brazil, _____ , India, _____ and South Africa.
> MINT = _____ , Indonesia, _____ and Turkey.

_____ ECONOMIES (NEEs)
— _____ getting _____ .
moving from _____ to _____ industry. E.g. the _____ and _____ countries.

 ☑ ☑ ☑

Measuring Development

Measures of Development

DEVELOPMENT —

GLOBAL DEVELOPMENT GAP —

Measure	What it is	= increases/decreases with development
Gross	Total value	
Birth rate		
	Deaths per	
Infant	No. of	
People per doctor		
	% adults	
Access to safe water		
Life expectancy		

Limitations of measures:

- **Variations**

Qatar's GNI per person is ....
— few extremely ....

- **Single**

Cuba has ....
but fairly ....

Classification by Wealth

HIGHER
(   )

E.g.

BRICS = ...

MINT = ...

LOWER
(   )
—   , very low
E.g.

NEWLY EMERGING
(   )
— rapidly

E.g. the   and   countries.

Measuring Development

The Human Development Index (HDI)

- Combines [_____] per head, life [_____] and [_____] level.
- Tells you about a country's [_____] and [_____] of life.
- Values between [____] and [____]. [____] = most developed
- Country classifications [_____] to [_____] per head.

Demographic Transition Model (DTM)

Shows how [_____] rates and [_____] rates affect [_____].

Birth rate [___] death rate ⟹ [_____] grows — [_____]

Death rate [___] birth rate ⟹ population [_____] — [_____]

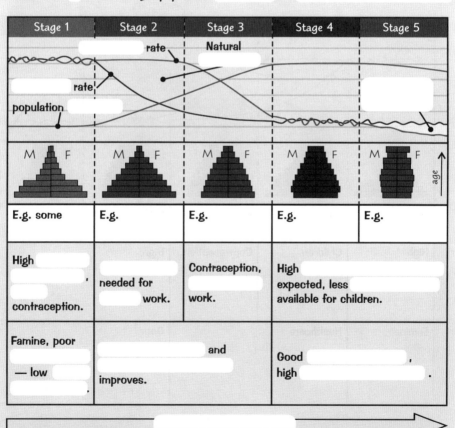

Stage 1	Stage 2	Stage 3	Stage 4	Stage 5
E.g. some	E.g.	E.g.	E.g.	E.g.
High [_____], contraception.	[_____] needed for [_____] work.	Contraception, [_____] work.	High [_____] expected, less available for children.	
Famine, poor [_____] — low [_____].	[_____] and [_____] improves.		Good [_____], high [_____].	

Measuring Development

The Human Development Index (HDI)

- Combines
- Tells you about a country's economic
- Values
- Country classifications

Demographic Transition Model (DTM)

Shows how _____ .

Birth rate > [_____] ➡ population [_____]

Death rate > [_____] ➡ population [_____]

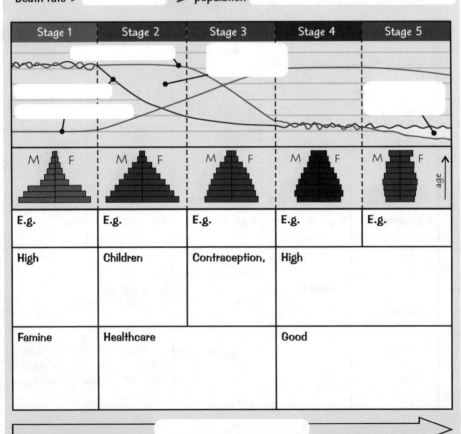

	Stage 1	Stage 2	Stage 3	Stage 4	Stage 5
E.g.	E.g.	E.g.	E.g.	E.g.	
High	Children	Contraception,	High	
Famine	Healthcare		Good	

Uneven Development

Physical Causes

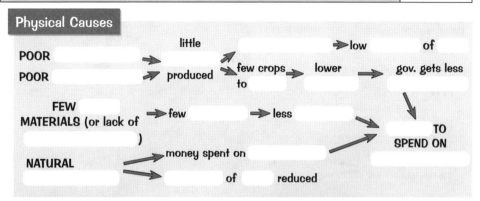

POOR ☐ → ☐ little → ☐ →low ☐ of ☐

POOR ☐ → produced few crops to → lower ☐ → gov. gets less

FEW ☐ MATERIALS (or lack of ☐) → few ☐ → less ☐ → ☐ TO SPEND ON ☐

NATURAL ☐ → money spent on ☐
→ ☐ of ☐ reduced

Economic Causes

POOR ☐ — Less trading = ☐ to spend on ☐ .

DEBT — ☐ money = ☐ to spend on ☐ .

☐ -PRODUCT ECONOMY — Low ☐ , fluctuating ☐ .

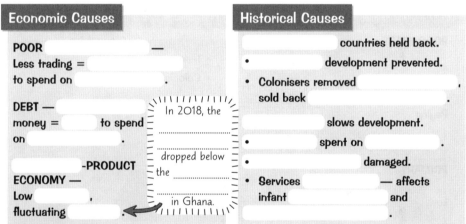

In 2018, the .... dropped below the .... in Ghana.

Historical Causes

☐ countries held back.
• ☐ development prevented.
• Colonisers removed ☐ , sold back ☐ .

☐ slows development.
• ☐ spent on ☐ .
• ☐ damaged.
• Services ☐ — affects infant ☐ and ☐ .

Consequences

WEALTH
Developed countries = ☐ .
More wealth = higher ☐ of ☐ .
☐ within countries too.

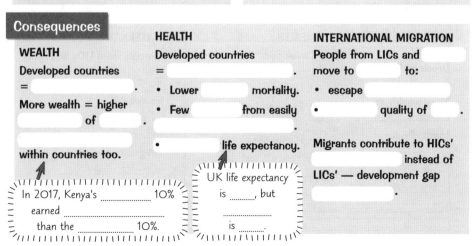

In 2017, Kenya's .... 10% earned .... than the .... 10%.

HEALTH
Developed countries = ☐ .
• Lower ☐ mortality.
• Few ☐ from easily ☐ .
• ☐ life expectancy.

UK life expectancy is ...., but .... is ....

INTERNATIONAL MIGRATION
People from LICs and ☐ move to ☐ to:
• escape ☐
• ☐ quality of ☐ .

Migrants contribute to HICs' ☐ instead of LICs' — development gap ☐ .

 ☑ ☑ ☑

Unit 2B — The Changing Economic World

Second Go:
..... / ..... / .....

Uneven Development

Physical Causes

POOR [____] → little → → → low
POOR [____] → → few → lower → gov. [____]

FEW [____]

(or [____] → few → less [____] ↘
[____]) → → → → **LESS** [____]

[____] → money
→ [____] of [____]

Economic Causes

POOR TRADE — [____]

— [____]
Paying

PRIMARY- — [____]

Low

In 2018, ...
....
....
....
....
....
....
....

Historical Causes

[____] countries [____] .

• Industry
• Colonisers

Conflict [____] .
• Money
•
• Services

Consequences

WEALTH
Developed

More wealth =
standard
Inequalities

In 2017, Kenya's ....
....
....

HEALTH
Developed

• Lower
• Few deaths from
• Higher life

UK life ....
....

INTERNATIONAL MIGRATION
People from LICs and NEEs

• escape
• improve

Migrants contribute

— development

 ☑ ☑ ☺ ☑

Reducing the Global Development Gap

Seven Strategies to Reduce the Gap

.... improved access
to water, healthcare and education
using UK .... in ....

1 FOREIGN-DIRECT INVESTMENT (FDI)

Foreign countries [   ] / invest.

- Access to [   ] / expertise.
- Improved [   ] / services.

3 .... TRADE

Farmers get a [   ] for goods.

- Fair Trade [   ] shows standards met.
- Buyers [   ] → help LIC's develop.
- Retailers may [   ] some extra profits.

5 .... LOANS

[   ] loans, e.g. for starting
[   ] / buying [   ].

Can encourage [   ].

7 DEBT [   ]

[   ] debt or lowering
[   ] rates.

Give LICs more to spend
on [   ].

2 AID

Money / [   ] for
[   ] provided by
[   ] or foreign government.

Aid money could be lost
_ [   ].

Projects [   ] if money [   ].

4 .... TECHNOLOGY

Tools, machines and systems
that improve [   ] of
but are [   ] and affordable to
buy / [   ].

6 .... DEVELOPMENT

Productivity, [   ] and
[   ] improved
→ boosts [   ] and [   ].

Zambia had .... of debt .... in 2005
— allowed them to start a free ....

Tourism and Development — Kenya

EXAMPLE

Kenya's ...., ...,
climate and scenery attracts tourists.

- [   ] income country in East [   ].
- Government boosted [   ] to increase development by [   ] visiting costs.
- [   ] fees cut and [   ] fees dropped →
  No. tourists increased from [   ] in 1995 to [   ] in 2017.

BENEFITS

Tourism = nearly [   ] of GDP
— improves [   ] /
[   ] of [   ].

Tourism employs > [   ] people.

Investment in transport [   ]
benefits [   ] and boosts [   ].

[   ] entry fees used to
protect [   ] and wildlife.

NEGATIVES

Money often goes to [   ] companies
— doesn't close [   ].

Maasai communities forced
to create [   ].

Vehicles destroy [   ] /
disturb [   ].

Tourist numbers [   ] —
[   ] source of jobs and [   ].

Second Go: ..... / ..... / ..... **Reducing the Global Development Gap**

Seven Strategies to Reduce the Gap

South Sudan improved access to

1 FOREIGN-DIRECT INVESTMENT (FDI)

Foreign countries
- Access to
- Improved

2 AID — Money / resources for

Aid money could

3 FAIR TRADE

Farmers get
- Fair Trade
- Buyers pay extra →
- Retailers may keep

4 INTERMEDIATE TECHNOLOGY

Tools, machines and systems that

5 MICROFINANCE LOANS

Small

6 INDUSTRIAL DEVELOPMENT

Productivity, skills and

7 DEBT RELIEF

Cancelling debt or

Zambia had ....
....
....

Tourism and Development — Kenya

Kenya's culture, wildlife, climate **EXAMPLE**
....
....

- Lower [   ] country in [   ] .
- Government [   ]
  to increase [   ] by reducing [   ] .
- Visa [   ] and [   ]
  → No. tourists increased from [   ] .

BENEFITS	NEGATIVES
Tourism =	Money often
Tourism employs >	Maasai communities
Investment in transport benefits	Vehicles destroy
National park protect	Tourist numbers

Mixed Practice Quizzes

Money might make the world go round, but revision's the only thing that'll help you learn everything from p.93-100. Try the quizzes, mark them and see how you did.

Quiz 1   Date: ...... / ...... / ......

1) Why are natural disasters likely to hold back a country's development?

2) Give three ways that an increase in tourism has benefited Kenya.

3) As a country develops, does the number of people per doctor increase or decrease?

4) Explain why debt relief can reduce the global development gap.

5) What is a Newly Emerging Economy?

6) Why is the birth rate in an undeveloped country likely to be high?

7) At Stage 2 of the DTM, is population increasing or decreasing?

8) Give an example of an HIC.

9) Explain how conflict can limit a country's development.

10) Explain why aid does not always succeed in reducing the development gap.

Total:

Quiz 2   Date: ...... / ...... / ......

1) What is 'Gross National Income per head'?

2) Give two reasons why birth rates might decrease when a country's economy shifts from agriculture towards manufacturing.

3) Give an example of aid given to reduce the development gap.

4) Which of the following measures increase with development? Death rate, life expectancy and / or GNI?

5) Give three physical factors that can hinder a country's development.

6) What HDI value would an extremely developed country have?

7) Give two reasons why people move from LICs to HICs.

8) Give three ways that a lack of development can affect people's health.

9) Give an example of a NEE.

10) How might foreign-direct investment benefit an LIC?

Total:

Mixed Practice Quizzes

Quiz 3   Date: ...... / ...... / ......

1) Give one change that Kenya made to boost its income from tourism. ☑

2) Which measure of development tells you the percentage of adults
   in a country that can read and write. ☑

3) How can international migration harm an LIC's development? ☑

4) What does NEE stand for? ☑

5) Why is the birth rate in a highly developed country usually low? ☑

6) Compare the birth rate and death rate of a country at Stage 5 of the DTM. ☑

7) Why might a previously colonised country be underdeveloped? ☑

8) How is a country's population likely to be changing
   if its death rate exceeds its birth rate? ☑

9) Give one advantage and one disadvantage of microfinance loans. ☑

10) Why is it helpful to look at several indicators
    when assessing a country's level of development? ☑

                                                        Total:

Quiz 4   Date: ...... / ...... / ......

1) Explain how poor farmland can affect a country's development. ☑

2) What is the 'global development gap'? ☑

3) True or false? A country with a high birth rate and a
   high infant mortality rate is likely to be well-developed. ☑

4) What measures are combined in the Human Development Index? ☑

5) Is the population pyramid shown on the right likely to   M ▮▮ F ↑
   represent a less developed or a more developed country?   age ☑

6) Why is a country with a primary-product economy
   likely to be less developed than other countries? ☑

7) What is intermediate technology? ☑

8) Give an example of an LIC. ☑

9) What causes a natural increase in population? ☑

10) What does the Fair Trade label show? ☑

                                                        Total:

Economic Development in India CASE STUDY

First Go: ..... / ..... / .....

A Rapidly Developing NEE

World's _____ largest pop. and still _____.

- Regionally important → links with _____ and _____.
- Globally important → exports _____ and _____ goods, member of _____ Organisation and _____.

Social	HDI = _____ — large inequalities / _____.
	Literacy rate < _____ — but _____.
Political	Former British _____ — now _____.
Environ-mental	Varied _____ — _____, Thar desert.
	_____ (Ganges & Indus) _____ land.
	Long _____ — attracts _____.
Cultural	Over 22 official _____. Religions include _____ and Islam.
	'_____' films / _____ dancing.

Changing Industrial Structure

GDP measures _____.

	Primary	Secondary	Tertiary	Quaternary
% GDP in/decreasing	~ _____ % decreasing	~ _____ %	_____	_____ %
% workforce	_____ %	24%		_____ %
Example			_____ (e.g. call centres)	_____ (e.g. IT)

Manufacturing industry:
- Stimulates _____ development.
- Provides _____ jobs (unlike seasonal _____ work).

Workers _____ income _____
Businesses _____ pay _____
attracted _____
_____ spends on _____

Transnational Corporations (TNCs)

TNCs build factories in _____ → cheap _____, fewer _____ = more _____.
TNC offices / _____ usually in _____ → more people with _____ skills.

Advantages for host:
- Employment
- TNCs pay _____.
- May run _____ programs.

Unilever employs _____ > _____ in India.

Disadvantages for host:
- Job _____ if factories _____ / relocate.
- Possible _____ problems.
- Pay and _____ may be _____.
- Some profits _____ India.

Unilever's _____ provides loans and saleable products to help poor women become _____.

Unilever is _____ → _____ may leave India.

 ☑   ☑ ☑

Economic Development in India

A Rapidly Developing NEE

World's second largest ....

- Regionally important →
- Globally important →

Social	HDI = Literacy rate <
Political	Former
Environ-mental	Varied landscape Long
Cultural	Over 22 official

Changing Industrial Structure

GDP ....

	Primary	Secondary	Tertiary	Quaternary
% GDP in/decreasing				
% workforce				
Example				

Manufacturing industry:
- Stimulates
- Provides reliable

Workers

Gov.

Transnational Corporations (TNCs)

TNCs build factories in LICs → ....

TNC offices / HQs usually in HICs → ....

Advantages for host:

Unilever employs ....

-
- TNCs
- May run

Unilever's Project Shakti provides loans

Disadvantages for host:
- Job losses if
- Possible
- Pay and
- Some

Unilever is ....

   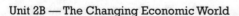

Economic Development in India

CASE STUDY

Changing Relationships with the Wider World

POLITICAL RELATIONSHIPS

- Tension with _____ and China over _____ .

- _____ built with other nations, e.g. the _____ policy increases India's _____ and regional security.

- _____ — will carry natural gas from _____ to India (through _____ and Pakistan).

TRADING RELATIONSHIPS

- Government reduced trade _____ , e.g.

- _____ agreements.

- _____ operating in India increase trade and _____ .

  E.g. _____ Trade Agreement with _____ , China, and Sri Lanka.

Aid Received

Type	How it works	Impacts	Example
SHORT-TERM	_____ / supplies for _____ .	Helps _____ — not _____ .	_____ provided supplies after _____ in N. India.
LONG-TERM	Investment in _____ projects.	Can improve infrastructure etc. Can be _____ , e.g. by _____ officials.	Until 2015, the _____ sent _____ per year for education, _____ & sanitation improvements.
TOP-DOWN	An _____ / _____ decides how to use aid.	Can improve _____ but may not help _____ , or be supported by _____	The _____ dam provides water / _____ , but _____ >300k people.
BOTTOM-UP	Given directly to _____ → they decide how to use it.	Improves _____ , skills and _____ in poor communities.	_____ trained to repair _____ in Gujarat → skills / improved _____ .

Impacts on Quality of Life

More _____ , increases in _____ water supply.

More _____ to _____ life, e.g. _____

HDI has _____ from 0.49 in 2000 to _____ .

Some jobs have _____ working conditions — reduced _____ of _____ .

Impacts on Environment

_____ fuels are most used, so: _____ energy consumption.

More _____ gas emissions and _____ .

_____ has world's worst _____ pollution.

Resource demand can destroy _____ .

But: people can _____ to spend more on the environment.

_____ mining damaged Bengal _____

CASE STUDY # Economic Development in India

Changing Relationships with the Wider World

POLITICAL RELATIONSHIPS
- Tension with

- Relationships built with

- TAPI pipeline —

TRADING RELATIONSHIPS
- Government reduced

- Free
- TNCs operating in

E.g. .... Trade Agreement
....

Aid Received

Type	How it works	Impacts	Example
SHORT-TERM	Money /	Helps	UNICEF
LONG-TERM	Investment	Can improve Can be	Until 2015, the UK & sanitation improvements.
TOP-DOWN	An organisation /	Can improve	The Sardar Sarovar
BOTTOM-UP	Given	Improves	Women trained / improved water supply.

Impacts on Quality of Life

| More jobs, | More money |

HDI has

Some jobs have

Impacts on Environment

.... fuels are most used, so:

Increasing ➡ More

and pollution.

Resource demand

But: people can afford to

.... has world's .... pollution.

Coal mining ....
....
....

Economic Development in the UK

Moving Towards a Post-Industrial Economy

[blank] → [blank] & Quaternary →

Important industries:
Services: e.g. [blank] ([blank] jobs).
[blank] : 670 000+ jobs.
Finance: [blank] in UK.
[blank] : £ [blank] spent in 2016.

Employed [blank] of workforce in [blank]

Near [blank] — researchers. ← SCIENCE & BUSINESS PARKS →

[blank] industries — develop technology.

↓ Increasing demand for [blank] products.

[blank] together → [blank] each other.

City [blank] — near housing & [blank] links.

Three Main Causes of Economic Change

⟨ % of GDP from [blank] trade increasing. ⟩

1 DE-INDUSTRIALISATION
[blank] → job losses.
[blank] goods from [blank] .

2 GLOBALISATION
Manufacturing moved [blank] — cheaper [blank] .
Some [blank] / quaternary operations moved to [blank] .

3 GOVERNMENT POLICIES
• 1980s: manufacturing industries [blank] → jobs lost but [blank] increased.
• [blank] (removing [blank] / taxes) → attracts [blank] to the UK.
• [blank] agreements / WTO membership → [blank] to operate across the [blank] .
↘ [blank] Organisation

Impacts on Environment

• [blank] / [blank] gases released, high energy / [blank] use.
• Modern industry more [blank] — increased energy and disposal costs, stricter [blank] .

The [blank] — EXAMPLE manufacturer in Lisburn, NI.
Increased [blank] — [blank] panels, 100% of [blank] from [blank] energy, [blank] boilers, leftover materials [blank] .

Transport Network

[blank] slows economic development.
• [blank] capacity — upgrades to [blank] motorways, e.g. [blank] .
• [blank] infrastucture, e.g. proposed [blank] — faster.
• [blank] capacity — third [blank] at Heathrow → noise / [blank] fears.
• [blank] capacity — London Gateway opened on [blank] in 2013 — can handle largest [blank] .

Economic Development in the UK

Moving Towards a Post-Industrial Economy

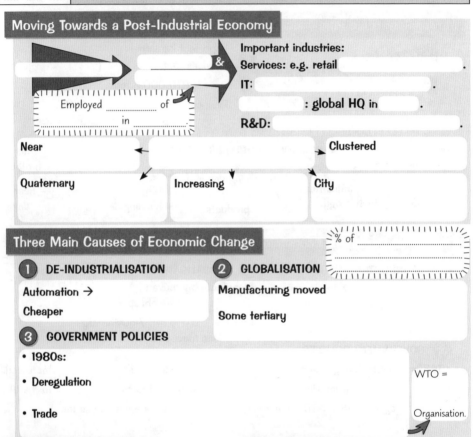

Employed _____ of _____ in _____.

Important industries:

Services: e.g. retail _____.

IT: _____.

_____ : global HQ in _____.

R&D: _____.

Near

Clustered

Quaternary

Increasing

City

Three Main Causes of Economic Change

% of _____

1 DE-INDUSTRIALISATION

Automation →

Cheaper

2 GLOBALISATION

Manufacturing moved

Some tertiary

3 GOVERNMENT POLICIES

• 1980s:

• Deregulation

• Trade

WTO = _____ Organisation.

Impacts on Environment

• Pollutants

_____ energy / water use.

• Modern industry more sustainable

_____ stricter regulations.

The Unicorn Group — manufacturer

Increased

_____ leftover materials recycled.

Transport Network

Congestion slows economic development.

• Road

• Rail

• Airport

• Port capacity — London Gateway opened on

Economic Development in the UK

Links to Other Countries

The UK left the .... in 2020. There's .... movement of goods / .... between EU member states.

Trade:
.... overseas .... per year.

Culture: exported ...., e.g. Aardman Animations.
.... shaped diverse UK culture, e.g. ....

Transport: .... Tunnel, ... = international hubs.

Electronic Communications: telephones / ....
.... cables routed via UK.

The Commonwealth —
.... states, many former UK .... Promotes co-operation and .... between members.

Change in Rural Areas

AREA	South Lakeland, Cumbria	North Somerset
POP. CHANGE		
REASONS	Job — .... / manufacturing.	Easy .... to Bristol.
ECONOMIC IMPACTS	.... closures, ... job	.... price rise, more ...., higher ....
SOCIAL IMPACTS	.... people moved away. .... population stayed.	Congestion, full ...., ... people move in.

Elderly pop. = strained .... / .... care.

Regional Differences

NORTH-SOUTH DIVIDE:
.... industry decline — .... impact on north.
.... industry growth
— mostly .... south.

.... for men born 2012 in: Glasgow = ... years, East Dorset = ... years.

.... / .... indicators (wages, health, GCSEs) tend to be .... in south.

Three approaches to resolving regional differences:

1 DEVOLUTION OF POWERS

Allows countries / local councils to use .... how they think best, e.g. improving public ...., ... projects.

2 ENTERPRISE ZONES

~ .... created across UK. Companies get .... for locating in zones:
• reduced ....
• simpler .... rules
• good ...., e.g. superfast broadband

.... Region Enterprise Zone has created .... jobs.

3 THE NORTHERN POWERHOUSE

Gov. plan to attract .... and improve .... in north.
Includes extending superfast .... and improving ....
But: often .... how money will be spent. Only focuses on ....

Economic Development in the UK

Links to Other Countries

Trade: £160bn
Culture: exported

Transport: Channel
Electronic communications:

The Commonwealth —
53 states, many former

Change in Rural Areas

AREA	South Lakeland, Cumbria	North Somerset
POP. CHANGE		
REASONS	Job	Easy
ECONOMIC IMPACTS	Shop	House
SOCIAL IMPACTS	Younger people	Congestion elderly

Elderly pop. = ...

Regional Differences

NORTH-SOUTH DIVIDE:

Life expectancy ....

Heavy industry

Service industry

Economic /

Three approaches to resolving regional differences:

1 DEVOLUTION OF POWERS

Allows countries /

2 ENTERPRISE ZONES

Sheffield ....
....
....

~50 created across UK.
Companies

• reduced
• simpler
• good   , e.g. superfast broadband.

3 THE NORTHERN POWERHOUSE

Gov. plan to attract investment and

But: often unclear how money

Mixed Practice Quizzes

Time for a quiz (or four) based on the content from p.103-110. Answer the questions, then mark the test yourself and see which topics need more development.

Quiz 1
Date: ...... / ...... / ......

1) Is India's population growing or shrinking? ☑
2) Give three examples of how the UK is attempting to reduce congestion in its transport network. ☑
3) What does 'devolution of powers' mean? ☑
4) Give two economic impacts of population decrease in rural areas of the UK. ☑
5) What is quaternary industry? ☑
6) Give two factors that influence the location of science and business parks. ☑
7) Give three main causes of economic change in the UK. ☑
8) Give two reasons why UK industry is more sustainable than it once was. ☑
9) Which sector of industry's GDP contribution is declining in India? ☑
10) What is short-term aid? ☑

Total: [ ]

Quiz 2
Date: ...... / ...... / ......

1) What factors contribute to the North-South divide in the UK? ☑
2) Why is India regionally important? ☑
3) Name a UK manufacturer that has greatly increased their sustainability. ☑
4) How has the UK's port capacity been increased? ☑
5) Give two reasons why TNCs often locate factories in LICs. ☑
6) Give three ways in which the UK is linked to other countries. ☑
7) Give an example of bottom-up aid. ☑
8) Give two reasons for de-industrialisation in the UK. ☑
9) Which sector of industry employs the greatest proportion of India's workforce? ☑
10) Give two ways India's trading relationships with the world have changed. ☑

Total: [ ]

Mixed Practice Quizzes

Quiz 3   Date: ...... / ...... / ......

1) Give two international organisations that India is a member of.
2) What is long-term aid meant to be used for?
3) What is promoted between Commonwealth members?
4) Which parts of TNCs usually locate in HICs?
5) Give an example of tertiary industry.
6) Give an advantage for a quaternary business of locating in a science and business park.
7) Describe the cultural significance of India.
8) In what decade were UK manufacturing industries privatised?
9) a) Why is a third runway planned for Heathrow?
   b) Why do some people object to a third runway?
10) How has India's HDI changed since 2000?

Total:

Quiz 4   Date: ...... / ...... / ......

1) Give two approaches to reducing the North-South divide in the UK.
2) Give one advantage and one disadvantage of top-down aid.
3) How has the UK government tried to attract investors to the UK?
4) True or false? India is an LIC.
5) How does manufacturing industry stimulate an economy?
6) a) Give three advantages to a country hosting a TNC factory.
   b) Give three disadvantages to a country hosting a TNC factory.
7) Why might a company want to locate in a UK Enterprise Zone?
8) Give three ways that the Unicorn Group increased their sustainability.
9) Give a social impact of population increase in a rural area of the UK.
10) Give an environmental impact of economic development in India.

Total:

Resources — Globally and in the UK

Vital Resources — Food, Water and Energy

FOOD —

Needed to avoid _____ (not getting enough food) and _____ (not getting the right balance of _____).

Malnourishment can limit children's _____ and increase _____ risk.

WATER —

Clean, safe water is needed for _____ , and _____ . _____ prevents the pollution of water sources by raw _____ , and water-borne _____ , e.g. _____ .

Needed to produce _____ such as _____ and _____ .

ENERGY —

Needed for _____ , and home use. Stable electricity supply = _____ quality of life.

No electricity → _____ / _____ used instead

→ deforestation / _____ .

Electricity can power _____ for _____ to provide safe water.

Unequal Resource Distribution

Global _____ and consumption is _____ . A country's _____ depends on:

1 RESOURCE AVAILABILITY — energy _____ , environment suited to food production.

2 WEALTH — to _____ resources, to _____ resources using _____ .

Country type	Consumption	Reason		
_____	High	Can _____ resources.	_____ standard of living.	
NEEs	_____	_____ —	and wealth increasing.	
_____	Low	_____ afford to _____	or _____ resources.	

Water in the UK

Demand is _____ — more _____ and larger population.

North and _____ ➡ _____ rainfall = water _____

South east and the _____ ➡ high _____ density = water deficit

Birmingham (....................) is supplied with water from Wales (....................).

Water _____ can be affected by pollution, e.g. from _____ , vehicles, _____ .

Strategies to manage water quality include:

• improving _____

• regulating _____ and _____ use.

Water can be _____ from areas of _____ to areas of _____ , but:

• building _____ and _____ is expensive.

• it affects _____ .

• it can cause _____ issues.

Resources — Globally and in the UK

Vital Resources — Food, Water and Energy

FOOD —

Needed to avoid

(not getting enough food)
and
(not
).

Malnourishment can limit

WATER —

Clean

Sanitation
of water sources

Needed to produce products
such as

ENERGY —

Needed for
and home use.

Stable electricity
= better quality

No electricity →

→ deforestation / .

Electricity

provide

Unequal Resource Distribution

Global supply and . A country's :

1 RESOURCE
AVAILABILITY —

2 WEALTH — to import

Country type	Consumption	Reason
HICs		of living.
	Industry	increasing.
	Low	Can't

Water in the UK

Demand is rising —

( ) is
supplied with water from
( ).

North and →
=

South east and the →
=

Water quality can be affected by
e.g. from fertilisers

Strategies to manage water quality include:

•

• regulating

Water can be

• building

•

• it can cause

Resources — Globally and in the UK

Food in the UK

_____ for certain types of food is _____ :

Organic food production is strictly ....

High-value foods
Often grown in _____ , e.g. _____ .
E.g. exotic fruits and vegetables, _____ , _____ •

Seasonal products
Out-of-season foods _____ .
E.g. in _____ , strawberries from _____ .

Organic produce
Increased _____ about:
• how _____ affect health.
• how food affects _____ .

BUT:

Imported food → _____ food miles → More _____ released → carbon + More environmental → Demand for _____ -sourced food

There is a growing trend towards _____ :
• large-scale _____ farms.
• more _____ used, e.g. _____ .
• more _____ = _____ workers needed.

CARBON FOOTPRINT (of food)
— the amount of _____ released while _____ and _____ food.

Energy in the UK

The _____ has changed:
• decreased _____ on fossil fuels (_____ , _____ and _____).
• greater _____ of renewables (wind, bioenergy, solar and hydroelectric power).

In .... , _____ generated .... % of UK electricity.

Aims to reduce _____ emissions → Decreased coal _____ → _____ drops | _____ sea oil and gas being used up _____ . → Extracting _____ through _____ is being considered.

_____ energy resources can cause issues:

Economic issues	Environmental issues
Extracting fossil fuels is _____ — cost increases as _____ used up.	_____ fossil fuels releases _____ and other _____ .
_____ and renewable energy is more _____ for consumers.	_____ may pollute _____ and cause _____ .
UK must _____ energy to meet _____ .	_____ disasters and damage the _____ .
_____ needed for _____ into _____ sources.	Renewable energy _____ damages _____ and may be an _____ .

Resources — Globally and in the UK

Food in the UK

_____

Demand _____

High-value foods
Often grown
e.g.
E.g.

Seasonal products

E.g. in winter,

Organic produce
Increased
• how   affect health.
• how food

BUT:

| | | More CO_2 released | | + environmental | | -sourced food increases |

There is a growing trend towards agribusiness:

•
• more chemicals
• more machinery

CARBON FOOTPRINT (of food) —

Energy in the UK

In 2014, ...

The energy
• decreased
• greater significance of renewables (, bioenergy,   and hydroelectric power).

Aims to   →   → Production

North Sea oil → Extracting shale

Exploiting energy resources can   :   being considered.

Economic issues	Environmental issues
Extracting fossil fuels	Burning
Nuclear is more	Fracking
UK must	Nuclear
Money	Renewable energy generation ecosystems and

Food Supply and Demand

Global Patterns of Food Supply and Calorie Intake

Food production:

North America and ⟶ (surplus)

and Africa ⟶ (deficit)

Country type	Daily ___ intake	
HICs	___ — more ___, more imports	
___	___ — less food, less ___	
___	Increasing — ___	

FOOD SECURITY — having access to enough ___ to stay ___ and ___.

FOOD INSECURITY — ___ having access to enough ___ to stay ___ and ___.

Two Reasons for Increase in Global Food Consumption

1 ___ population: More people ___.

2 Economic development:
- ___ countries can buy and import ___ food.
- ___ agriculture — food is ___.

Factors Affecting Food Supply

PHYSICAL
- Climate and extreme ___.
- Water ___ — low ___ or little water for ___.
- ___ and ___ reduce crop ___.

HUMAN
- ___ — harder to ___, ___ and import food.
- Technology — e.g. ___ makes farming more ___.
- Conflict — ___ farmland, unsafe ___, political relationships ___.

Impacts of Food Insecurity

FAMINE — widespread ___ of ___ Can lead to ___ and ___.

UNDERNUTRITION — not eating enough ___ to stay healthy.

Stunted ___ affects ~ ___ of children under five in sub-Saharan Africa.

SOIL EROSION — over- ___ and ___ damages farmland.

RISING FOOD PRICES — demand ___ supply → higher prices → further ___.

SOCIAL UNREST — food ___ and high food ___ can lead to looting, ___ and ___.

Food Supply and Demand

Global Patterns of Food Supply and Calorie Intake

Food production:

➡️

➡️

Country type	Daily calorie intake
	Higher
	Lower

FOOD SECURITY —

FOOD INSECURITY —

Two Reasons for Increase in Global Food Consumption

1. Rising population:

2. Economic development:
   - Wealthier countries can
   - •

Factors Affecting Food Supply

PHYSICAL
- Climate and
- Water

- Pests

HUMAN
- Poverty — and import food.
- Technology — e.g. machinery makes farming
- Conflict —

Impacts of Food Insecurity

FAMINE — widespread lack of
Can lead to

UNDERNUTRITION —

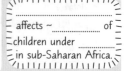
....
affects ~ .... of
children under ....
in sub-Saharan Africa.

SOIL EROSION —
and   damages farmland.

RISING FOOD PRICES —

SOCIAL UNREST — food shortages and

and civil wars.

Increasing Food Production

Five Strategies to Increase Food Supply

1 IRRIGATION

Artificially [   ] land in
dry areas → [   ].

- [   ] —
  ditches and channels.
- Sprinklers
- Drip systems —
  [   ] in pipes.

2 HYDROPONICS AND AEROPONICS

Growing plants without [   ].
[   ], but uses [   ] and
lower disease / pest risk = less need for [   ].

HYDROPONICS — plants grown
in [   ].

AEROPONICS — plants [   ] in air.
Water containing nutrients [   ] onto [   ].

3 BIOTECHNOLOGY

Involves [   ] modified (GM) crops.
Increased [   ], [   ] value, and
[   ] to pests, disease and drought.
But — environmental and [   ] concerns ,
e.g. reduced [   ], disrupted ecosystems.

4 NEW GREEN REVOLUTION

Increases yields [   ] using:

- [   ]
- Traditional / organic methods,
  e.g. [   ],
  [   ].

5 [   ] TECHNOLOGY

Methods [   ] to the local environment
and people, e.g. their [   ] and [   ].

E.g. using an irrigation system
constructed from [............................]
is more [............................] than an
imported, [............................] system.

Burkina Faso — Large Scale Agricultural Development

EXAMPLE

Burkina Faso is an [   ] in [   ].

PROBLEMS:
Hot, dry, [   ] rainy
season → [   ].
[   ] population→
malnutrition, food [   ].

RESPONSE:
[   ], [   ] and
canals built to provide
reliable water supply
for [   ].

Burkina
Faso

The [............] Dam stores
[............] billion m³ of water.

ADVANTAGES

- [   ] water supply from
  [   ] irrigation systems.
- [   ] fields created — rice grown.
- More than [   ] created.
- Dam is used for [   ].

DISADVANTAGES

- Only irrigated [   ] of planned area.
- Water [   ] — canals not [   ].
- Water too [   ] for most farmers.
- People [   ] and land [   ].
- Opening dams can cause [   ].

Increasing Food Production

Five Strategies to Increase Food Supply

1 IRRIGATION

Artificially

→ better yields.

- Gravity

-

- Drip

2 HYDROPONICS AND AEROPONICS

Growing plants   . Expensive but

HYDROPONICS —

AEROPONICS — plants suspended
Water containing

3 BIOTECHNOLOGY

Involves genetically modified

and resistance to pests,

But — environmental and
e.g. reduced biodiversity,

4 NEW GREEN REVOLUTION

Increases yields sustainably using:

-

- Traditional / organic methods

5 APPROPRIATE TECHNOLOGY

Methods suited to the local
and people, e.g. their

E.g. using an _____
constructed from _____
is more _____ than an
_____ system.

Burkina Faso — Large Scale Agricultural Development

EXAMPLE

Burkina Faso is an LIC in West Africa.

PROBLEMS:
Hot

Rising

RESPONSE:
Dams,

....
....
....
....

ADVANTAGES

-

gravity-based

- Paddy fields created —

- More than

- Dam is used for

DISADVANTAGES

- Only   of planned area.

- Water loss —

- Water too expensive for most

- People

- Opening dams

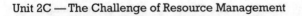

Sustainable Food Supply

Low Impact Food Production

Type	What it involves
....	• Natural processes return .... to soil. • Pesticides and animal .... restricted → .... protected. • Crops rotated, natural .... → less environmental damage. • Sold near farm — ....
PERMACULTURE	• Natural ecosystems .... — protects .... and .... • .... — better use of .... / light, fewer pests / diseases, less .... • Natural predators → fewer pesticides needed.
URBAN FARMING INITIATIVES	• Farming in towns, e.g. .... • .... — less food miles. • Cheaper — improves ....
SUSTAINABLY SOURCED FISH AND MEAT	• .... — avoid overfishing. • Environmentally-friendly fishing methods. • Locally-sourced .... • Eating all .... parts of animals. • Seaweed in cattle feed — decreased ....

Industrial agriculture uses .... of world's .... supplies.

Urban farming reduces dependence on ....

Sustainable Consumption

Eat .... food, not imported food.

Reduced ....

↓

Reduced ....

↓

Lower .... — these contribute to ....

.... less food.

Encouraged by schemes like '............ '.

Supermarkets can help distribute .... to those in need.

LIC Sustainability Scheme

• Mali is a .... LIC.
• Intensive farming → desertification → ....
• Farmers use .... to grow .... between other plants:

Trees — .... and wind protection, prevent .... erosion

Leaf litter — .... and nutrient content ....

Maize

Nitrogen .... plants add nitrogen to soil

• Maize yield ....
• Soil protected → ....

Sustainable Food Supply

Low Impact Food Production

.... uses .... of world's .... supplies.

Type	What it involves
ORGANIC FARMING	• Natural • Pesticides → • Crops rotated, natural → less environmental damage •
PERMACULTURE	• Natural ecosystems recreated — • Mixed cropping — • Natural predators → fewer
URBAN FARMING INITIATIVES	• Farming in • Local • Cheaper —
SUSTAINABLY SOURCED FISH AND MEAT	• Catch quotas — • Environmentally-friendly • Locally-sourced • Eating • Seaweed in

Urban farming reduces .... on ....

Sustainable Consumption

Eat

⬇

⬇

Lower

Waste less food.

Encouraged by

Supermarkets

LIC Sustainability Scheme

• Mali
• Intensive   → desertification
  →
• Farmers use
  grow maize between

Leaf litter   Trees —

Maize

Nitrogen   fixing plants
     add   to soil

•
• Soil

Mixed Practice Quizzes

Time to check how much information you've consumed from p.113-122 by trying out the surplus of quiz questions below. Don't worry — they're sustainably sourced.

Quiz 1   Date: ...... / ...... / ......

1) Name three resources that are vital for humans.
2) Why are there fewer workers in agribusiness than in traditional agriculture?
3) Define 'food security'.
4) How does the industrialisation of agriculture help to increase global food consumption?
5) How can conflict affect food supply?
6) a) What type of fuels is the UK energy mix shifting away from?
   b) What type of resources are becoming more significant in the UK?
7) Give an advantage of aeroponics.
8) What does 'undernourishment' mean?
9) Give two disadvantages of building dams and reservoirs in Burkina Faso.
10) How might food insecurity lead to soil erosion?

Total:

Quiz 2   Date: ...... / ...... / ......

1) Give a reason why coal production in the UK has decreased.
2) State two effects of malnourishment.
3) True or false? HICs have a higher calorie intake than LICs.
4) Explain why sanitation is vital to health.
5) Name four impacts of food insecurity.
6) Why is the demand for locally-sourced food increasing?
7) Give three advantages of using biotechnology to produce GM crops.
8) Give two advantages of building dams and reservoirs in Burkina Faso.
9) a) True or false? Agroforestry involves growing crops between other plants.
   b) How has agroforestry benefitted farming in Mali?
10) Give three physical factors that affect food supply.

Total:

Mixed Practice Quizzes

Quiz 3 Date: ...... / ...... / ......

1) Give two factors that affect a country's resource consumption.
2) Give two reasons why water demand is rising in the UK.
3) How might water stress affect food supply?
4) What is a food's 'carbon footprint'?
5) Describe resource consumption in HICs, LICs and NEEs.
6) Give two reasons why global food consumption is increasing.
7) What is the difference between hydroponics and aeroponics?
8) Give two environmental problems that may be caused by fracking.
9) Define 'appropriate technology'.
10) a) Name a part of the world that produces a surplus of food.
    b) Name a part of the world with deficient food production.

Total:

Quiz 4 Date: ...... / ...... / ......

1) Why is it becoming increasingly expensive to extract fossil fuels?
2) Give three human factors that affect food supply.
3) How does the New Green Revolution increase crop yields?
4) Give one reason why the west of the UK generally has a water surplus.
5) Why does Burkina Faso suffer from food insecurity?
6) State two strategies for managing water quality.
7) Give two features of permaculture.
8) Give an example of how technology can affect food supply.
9) Why might it be better to eat locally-sourced food
   instead of imported food?
10) Where are high-value foods usually produced?

Total:

Water Supply and Demand

Global Patterns of Water Security / Insecurity

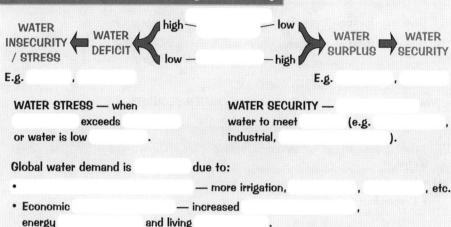

WATER INSECURITY / STRESS ← WATER DEFICIT ← high ——[   ]—— low → WATER SURPLUS → WATER SECURITY

low ——[   ]—— high

E.g. [   ] ,   E.g. [   ] ,

WATER STRESS — when [   ] exceeds [   ] or water is low [   ].

WATER SECURITY — [   ] water to meet [   ] (e.g. [   ], industrial, [   ]).

Global water demand is [   ] due to:

• [   ] — more irrigation, [   ], [   ], etc.
• Economic [   ] — increased [   ], energy [   ] and living [   ].

Factors Affecting Water Availability

PHYSICAL:

<u>Climate</u>
• Rainfall is needed to [   ].
• Higher temp → more water [   ].

<u>Geology</u>

Ran runs off [   ] rock

[   ] to get water from rivers and lakes.

Ran infiltrates [   ] rock

Hard to get water from [   ] stores.

SOCIO-ECONOMIC:

Over-abstraction — water used [   ] water replaced.

[   ] — e.g. by industry or animal waste.

Limited infrastructure — too few [   ] / [   ].

[   ] — people can't afford water provider fees.

Water Insecurity Impacts

POLLUTION & DISEASE — using [   ] water can lead to [   ], e.g. [   ].

REDUCED FOOD PRODUCTION — insufficient [   ] reduces [   ], leading to [   ].

REDUCED INDUSTRIAL OUTPUT — less [   ] = less [   ]. Economy affected, incomes [   ].

CONFLICT — can occur when countries [   ] a [   ].

Actions of [   ] countries affect countries [   ].

Water Supply and Demand

Global Patterns of Water Security / Insecurity

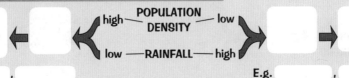

high — **POPULATION DENSITY** — low

low — **RAINFALL** — high

E.g. _____ , _____

E.g. _____ , _____

WATER STRESS —

WATER SECURITY —

Global
- Increasing
- Economic

Factors Affecting Water Availability

PHYSICAL:

<u>Climate</u>
- Rainfall is needed to
- Higher temp →

<u>Geology</u>

 Easy

 Hard

aquifer

SOCIO-ECONOMIC:

Over-abstraction — water used

Pollution — e.g. by

Limited infrastructure — too few

Poverty — people can't

Water Insecurity Impacts

POLLUTION & DISEASE —
using

REDUCED FOOD PRODUCTION
— insufficient

REDUCED INDUSTRIAL OUTPUT
— less water =

CONFLICT —
can occur

Increasing Water Supply

Four Ways to Increase Water Supply

1 Building a _____ across a river _____ water, creating a **RESERVOIR**. Water is _____ when there's a _____.
But: _____ farmland and forces people to _____. Expensive.

2 **WATER DIVERSION** — a dam raises a river's _____ and _____ water for _____ or _____.
No reservoir so _____ disruptive than a storage dam.

3 **WATER TRANSFER SCHEMES** — large-scale _____ projects that move water from areas of _____ to areas of _____.
But: can cause _____ problems (see below). _____.

4 **DESALINATION** removes _____ from seawater either by _____ and condensation, or by passing it through a _____. Used by wealthy _____ countries.
But: requires lots of _____. Expensive.

> Desalination supplies _____ of Dubai's water.

South-North Water Transfer Project — China

EXAMPLE

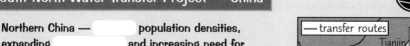

Northern China — _____ population densities, expanding _____ and increasing need for _____ land = high _____ for water.
Leads to _____. 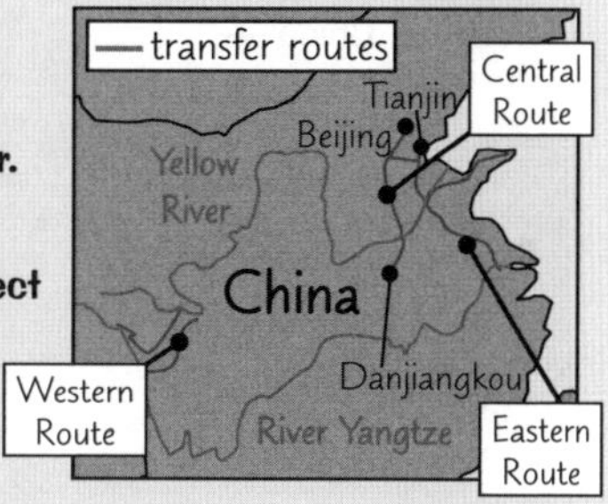
Government planned a _____ water project to transfer _____ billion m³ of water yearly:
- Cost _____.
- Work began in _____.
- Central and _____ completed by 2014.
- _____ Route's completion planned for _____.

Map labels: transfer routes · Central Route · Tianjin · Beijing · Yellow River · China · Danjiangkou · Western Route · River Yangtze · Eastern Route

ADVANTAGES:
- Clean water for over _____ cities.
- Up to _____ may benefit.
- Allows _____ development to continue in the _____.
- Water provided for _____.
- Prevents _____, reducing land _____.

DISADVANTAGES:
- Flooding destroyed _____.
- _____ harms ecosystems.
- More water stress / _____ in south.
- _____ flooded, _____ people relocated with little _____.
- Water supplied to Beijing is _____ and only available in _____.

Second Go:
..... /..... /.....

Increasing Water Supply

Four Ways to Increase Water Supply

1 Building a STORAGE DAM

But:

2 WATER DIVERSION —

3 WATER TRANSFER SCHEMES —

But:

4 DESALINATION

But:

South-North Water Transfer Project — China

EXAMPLE

Northern China —

Government planned

- Cost
- Work began
- Central
- Western

ADVANTAGES:
- Clean water for

- Up to

- Allows

- Water
- Prevents

DISADVANTAGES:
- Flooding

- Construction

- More water

- Farmland flooded

- Water supplied to Beijing is

Unit 2C — The Challenge of Resource Management

 ☑ ☑ ☑

Sustainable Water Supply

Sustainable Strategies to Increase Water Supply

.... of water in the UK is lost to ....

Strategy	What it involves
WATER CONSERVATION	• Fix .... in reservoirs, pipes and .... • Use .... toilets, washing machines, ... , etc. • .... to where water is .... • Increase awareness of costs, e.g. fit ....
GROUNDWATER MANAGEMENT	• Monitor .... / pass .... to prevent over-abstraction. • Avoid .... and fine companies that leak .... waste. • Create international agreements to share groundwater sustainably.
....	• Wastewater piped to .... to make safe for reuse. • Most recycled water used for .... , industry, power plants and toilet flushing — but it can be treated further for ....
' .... ' **WATER**	• Water that is reused .... treatment. • Mostly .... wastewater (NOT from toilets — contaminated). • Clean enough for irrigation and flushing toilets, ... for drinking. • Saves .... used in .... • Systems expensive. Water must be used .... (bacteria grow).

Increasing Sustainable Water Supplies — Kenya

EXAMPLE

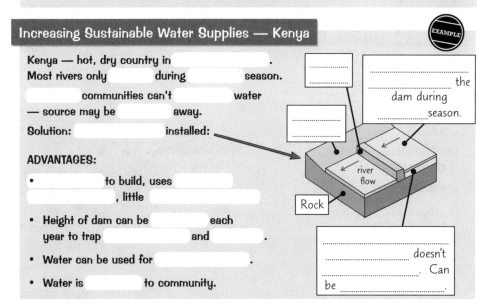

Kenya — hot, dry country in ....
Most rivers only .... during .... season.
.... communities can't .... water
— source may be .... away.
Solution: .... installed:

....
....

.... the dam during .... season.

....

ADVANTAGES:

• .... to build, uses .... , little ....

• Height of dam can be .... each year to trap .... and ....

• Water can be used for ....

• Water is .... to community.

← river flow

Rock

.... doesn't .... Can be ....

 ✓ ✓ ✓ Unit 2C — The Challenge of Resource Management

Sustainable Water Supply

Sustainable Strategies to Increase Water Supply

> .... of water in the
> UK is ....

Strategy	What it involves
WATER CONSERVATION	• Fix • Use efficient • • Increase
GROUNDWATER MANAGEMENT	• Monitor pass laws to prevent . • Avoid fertilisers and fine companies • Create international agreements to groundwater sustainably.
RECYCLING	• Wastewater piped to treatment plants to • Most recycled water used for — but it can be treated further for drinking.
'GREY' WATER	• Water that is • Mostly domestic wastewater • Clean enough for • Saves • Systems expensive. Water must be used quickly (grow).

Increasing Sustainable Water Supplies — Kenya

EXAMPLE

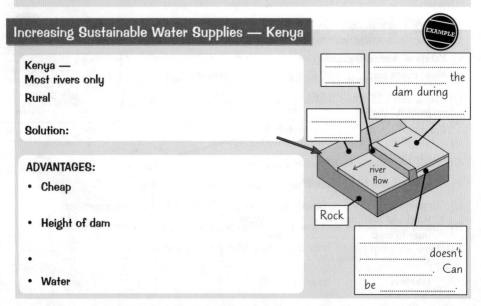

Kenya —
Most rivers only
Rural

Solution:

ADVANTAGES:

• Cheap

• Height of dam

•

• Water

.... the
dam during
....

....

river flow

Rock

.... doesn't
.... Can
be ....

 ✓ ✓ ✓

Mixed Practice Quizzes

Yep, it's that time again. These quizzes flow nicely on from what you've learnt on p.125-130. If you're thirsty for more revision, I'm sure this will whet your appetite.

Quiz 1   Date: ...... / ...... / ......

1) Why does poverty make clean water unavailable to some people?
2) Give two examples of what groundwater management may involve.
3) Does a high or low population density lead to water insecurity?
4) Explain what is meant by 'water diversion'.
5) Give two physical factors that affect water availability.
6) Why must grey water be used quickly?
7) Define 'water stress'.
8) Give two ways that China's South-North Water Transfer Project has benefitted people.
9) Give an example of how a water company can conserve water.
10) How can water insecurity lead to disease?

Total:

Quiz 2   Date: ...... / ...... / ......

1) Define 'water security'.
2) Why do higher temperatures contribute to water insecurity?
3) How does building a storage dam across a river increase water supply?
4) What is 'desalination'?
5) How does a sand dam store water?
6) Give four impacts of water insecurity.
7) True or false? Recycled water can be used for drinking.
8) Explain why China's South-North Water Transfer Project was needed.
9) Does high rainfall and low population lead to a water surplus or deficit?
10) Give an example of how a householder can conserve water.

Total:

Mixed Practice Quizzes

Quiz 3   Date: ...... / ...... / ......

1) Give two reasons why global water demand is increasing.

2) Give a disadvantage of building a storage dam.

3) How does China's South-North Water Transfer Project reduce land subsidence?

4) Name a country that suffers from water insecurity.

5) Give two uses of recycled water.

6) How can water insecurity affect a country's economy?

7) What is 'grey water'?

8) How does the geology of an area affect water availability?

9) Give an advantage of a sand dam.

10) Give two ways that climate affects water availability.

Total:

Quiz 4   Date: ...... / ...... / ......

1) Name a water-secure country.

2) How can water insecurity lead to starvation?

3) Give two methods of desalination.

4) Why is water diversion less disruptive than building a storage dam?

5) Explain why a shared water source can lead to conflict.

6) True or false? A sand dam only works for one year.

7) What is 'over-abstraction'?

8) Give two ways that China's South-North Water Transfer Project has negatively affected people.

9) Why does economic development increase water demand?

10) Give two uses of grey water.

Total:

Energy Supply and Demand

First Go:
..... / ..... / .....

Energy Security

ENERGY SECURITY — having a
reliable, _____ and
_____ supply of energy

ENERGY SURPLUS —
having _____ energy than
the population requires.

ENERGY DEFICIT —
having _____ energy than
the population requires.

A country's _____ depends on:
- available _____
- _____ size
- average _____ per _____

Global Patterns of Production and Consumption

_____ reserves + ability to _____ ➡ _____ production, e.g. Iran, China, Russia

_____ reserves / inability to _____ ➡ _____ production, e.g. _____, Sudan

_____ ➡ _____ standard of living ➡ Use _____ heating, _____ ➡ _____ energy consumption

_____ ➡ _____ standard of living ➡ Lifestyles less _____ ➡ _____ energy consumption

Factors Affecting Supply

PHYSICAL:
Amount of reserves and _____ of extraction.
Suitability for renewables (_____ / geology).
Likelihood of _____.

TECHNOLOGICAL ADVANCES:
_____ / easier to exploit _____ /
existing resources, e.g. _____.

ECONOMIC:
_____ reserves more costly to extract.
Fuel sometimes _____ for LICs.
LICs may lack _____ to exploit reserves or
build energy _____.

POLITICAL:
Political instability
affects _____.
Stricter _____ regulations.
International _____ agreements.

The _____ East's oil
exports _____
during the Gulf War.

Rising Energy Demand

_____ —
more people = more energy needed.
ECONOMIC DEVELOPMENT —
more _____, more _____ =
more _____ -using goods bought.
TECHNOLOGICAL ADVANCES —
new _____ need _____.

Impacts of Energy Insecurity

_____ DAMAGE —
reserves in sensitive areas exploited.
FOOD SHORTAGES —
struggle to _____
_____ equipment.
INDUSTRIAL OUTPUT —
reduced _____ → _____ lost,
_____ prices for consumers.
CONFLICT — between areas of
_____ and areas of _____.

Second Go: ..... /..... /.....	**Energy Supply and Demand**

Energy Security

ENERGY SECURITY — having

supply of energy.

ENERGY SURPLUS —

ENERGY DEFICIT —

A country's energy security depends on:
- available
-
- average use per

Global Patterns of Production and Consumption

Large reserves + ➡ high production, e.g.

Few reserves / ➡ low production, e.g.

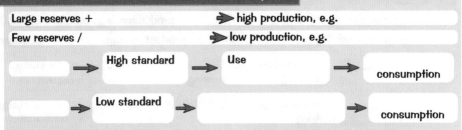

➡ High standard ➡ Use ➡ consumption

➡ Low standard ➡ ➡ consumption

Factors Affecting Supply

PHYSICAL:

Amount of reserves and ease of

Suitability for (climate / geology).

Likelihood

TECHNOLOGICAL ADVANCES:

Possible / easier

ECONOMIC:

Depleted reserves to extract.

Fuel sometimes too

LICs may lack funds to

The Middle East's

POLITICAL:

Stricter

International agreements.

Rising Energy Demand

RISING POPULATION — more people
=

ECONOMIC DEVELOPMENT —
more industry,
more energy-using

TECHNOLOGICAL ADVANCES —
new

Impacts of Energy Insecurity

ENVIRONMENTAL DAMAGE —
in sensitive areas exploited.

FOOD SHORTAGES —
struggle

INDUSTRIAL OUTPUT —
reduced
for consumers.

CONFLICT — between areas of

Increasing Energy Supplies

Renewable Energy Sources

Type	Overview	Example
SOLAR	Water heaters are _____ . Photovoltaic cells are expensive — but excess energy can be _____ . _____ — not always _____ .	_____ , Morocco. Supplies _____ people.
HYDRO (...............)	Dammed water _____ and turns _____ . _____ output. Expensive. _____ loss.	The Three Gorges Dam, _____ .
GEO-THERMAL	Water pumped underground → _____ . Steam turns _____ or heats _____ . Cheap, reliable, best in _____ active areas.	Supplies _____ of _____ home heating and hot water.
....	_____ / water level changes turn _____ . Reliable. _____ , variable _____ .	_____ Swansea Bay _____ Lagoon.
....	Waves turn _____ . _____ .	Testing in _____ .
WIND	No _____ emissions once _____ . Unreliable.	_____ : Denmark ran on wind power for a _____ .
BIOMASS	Plants / animal waste → burnt / make _____ . _____ technology needed — good for _____ . Renewable if _____ managed.	_____ produced _____ barrels of biofuel a day in 2015.

Non-Renewable Sources

FOSSIL FUELS

Reserves _____ / become too _____ to extract. BUT:

- _____ reserves may be _____ .

- _____ allows extraction of previously _____ reserves.

NUCLEAR POWER

_____ will run out, but:

- New _____ increases _____ .

- New _____ reactors. generate more _____ .

Fracking

EXAMPLE

FRACKING — liquid pumped into _____ rock at _____ , rock _____ to release _____ .

PROS:

_____ UK reserves — increases energy _____ .

Less _____ than other fossil fuels.

_____ than some renewables.

CONS:

_____ sustainable — high water use, gas is non- _____ burning it releases _____ .

May pollute _____ and _____ .

May cause small _____ .

May _____ investment in renewable energy.

.... near .... halted in .... due to .... concerns.

 ☑ ☑ 😊 ☑ Unit 2C — The Challenge of Resource Management

Increasing Energy Supplies

Renewable Energy Sources

Type	Overview	Example
SOLAR	Water heaters	Supplies
HYDRO (HEP)	Adjustable output	
GEO-THERMAL	Steam Cheap, reliable, in tectonically areas.	Supplies 87% of
TIDAL	Reliable.	Proposed
WAVE	Waves	
WIND	No	2017:
BIOMASS	Plants / animal waste → Little Renewable	USA produce 1m in 2015.

Non-Renewable Sources

FOSSIL FUELS
Reserves run out / become
                    to extract.
BUT:
- New

- Technology

NUCLEAR POWER

BUT:
- New

- New breeder

Fracking

FRACKING —

PROS:
Huge UK reserves — increases
Less
Cheaper

CONS:
Not

Fracking near
....
....
....

May pollute
May cause
May slow down investment in

Sustainable Energy

Sustainable Energy and Carbon Footprints

SUSTAINABLE ENERGY — provide energy _____ without preventing _____ generations from meeting _____.

Important because:
- Energy demand _____ with population.
- _____ _____ resources running out.

Humans must:
- exploit _____ resources
- find new _____ sources
- use _____ efficiently

CARBON FOOTPRINT — amount of _____ a person's _____ produce. Includes _____ and _____ emissions.

.... emissions — from things that .... energy, e.g. ....
.... emissions — from ....
things we ...., e.g. ....

Energy Conservation

Sustainable _____:
- _____ buildings.
- Fit efficient _____ and _____ panels.
- Use electric _____.
- Use _____ vehicles.

_____ Reduction:
- _____ to reduce energy use — e.g. _____ relief, _____ charges.
- _____ transport improvements.
- _____ meters → _____ of use.

Use Technology to Increase _____:
- Energy saving _____.
- _____ vehicles.
- _____ braking — storing energy _____ when braking.
- Make _____ more efficient.
- Combined Cycle Gas Turbine technology in _____ stations. — lost _____ recovered and used to generate more _____.

Renewable Energy in Bihar, India (an NEE)

EXAMPLE

_____ electricity supply — _____ of people not connected to grid.

In _____, _____ used to supply electricity:
- Local _____ used — a _____ product.
- Small, _____ power plants — _____.
- Electricity supplied to homes in _____ range.

This scheme was ....
.... — the rice husks and electricity don't ....

- By 2015, _____ rice husk power plants in Bihar → electricity for _____.
- Less need for diesel _____ / kerosene _____ → reduced fossil fuel use.
- Local people _____ → creates _____ and more sustainable.

Second Go: ..... /..... /.....

Sustainable Energy

Sustainable Energy and Carbon Footprints

SUSTAINABLE ENERGY —

Important because:

- Energy

- Non-renewable

Humans must:
- exploit
- find
- use

CARBON FOOTPRINT —

.... — from things that .... , e.g. .... emissions — from .... things we .... , e.g. ....

Energy Conservation

Sustainable Design:
-
- Fit efficient
- Use electric
- Use

Demand Reduction:
- Incentives to
-
- Public
- Smart meters →

Use Technology to Increase Efficiency:
-
- Hybrid
- Regenerative

- Make engines
- Combined Cycle Gas Turbine technology in power stations —

Renewable Energy in Bihar, India (an NEE)

Unreliable electricity supply — EXAMPLE

- Local rice husks used —
- Small, local power
- Electricity supplied to homes in

This scheme was very .... — the rice husks and ....

- By 2015, rice husk power plants in Bihar → electricity for
- Less need for → reduced
- Local people

Unit 2C — The Challenge of Resource Management

Mixed Practice Quizzes

It's almost time to wave goodbye to this section, but not before you use your energy surplus to answer these tidally awesome quizzes based on p.133-138.

Quiz 1   Date: ...... / ...... / ......

1) Give an example of how politics can affect energy supply.
2) Why is biomass a useful energy source for LICs?
3) What is 'energy security'?
4) a) Outline how electricity is produced in HEP.
   b) Give an advantage of using HEP.
5) Give an advantage of using shale gas over other fossil fuels.
6) How might smart meters reduce energy demand?
7) Give an example of an NEE that uses biomass to generate electricity.
8) What is meant by a person's 'carbon footprint'?
9) Explain why economic development results in increasing energy demand.
10) Outline what Combined Cycle Gas Turbine technology does in a power station.

Total:

Quiz 2   Date: ...... / ...... / ......

1) What does it mean if a country has an energy surplus?
2) Give an example of a country that uses a lot of geothermal energy.
3) Give three impacts of energy insecurity.
4) What is 'sustainable energy'?
5) Why do wealthy countries consume a large amount of energy?
6) Give one way that a government can reduce demand for energy.
7) Give two factors that can affect a country's ability to produce energy.
8) True or false? Biofuel is always renewable.
9) Give two reasons why energy demand is rising.
10) Give an environmental problem associated with fracking.

Total:

Mixed Practice Quizzes

Quiz 3   Date: ...... / ...... / ......

1) Name four types of renewable energy.
2) Give three physical factors that can affect energy supply.
3) Why might the amount of fossil fuels available for use increase?
4) What is the difference between 'direct' greenhouse gas emissions and 'indirect' greenhouse gas emissions?
5) What is an 'energy deficit'?
6) Why are rice husks an efficient choice of raw material for energy production in Bihar, India?
7) Why might energy insecurity result in food shortages?
8) Give three ways that humans can make energy use more sustainable.
9) Why might a country produce little energy despite having large reserves?
10) What is fracking?

Total:

Quiz 4   Date: ...... / ...... / ......

1) How can technological advances increase energy supply?
2) Name two unreliable renewable energy resources.
3) Why might energy insecurity result in environmental damage?
4) Give two advantages for the UK of fracking to produce energy.
5) Give two ways that uranium supplies are being conserved.
6) What is regenerative braking?
7) Give three things that a country's energy security depends on.
8) What is normally used to produce biofuels?
9) Is fracking sustainable? Explain your answer.
10) Name a country that has large energy reserves and is able to exploit them.

Total:

Fieldwork

First Go: ..... /..... /.....

Data Collection

PRIMARY DATA — collected by [____].

SECONDARY DATA — collected by [____].

You start with a research question / [____] — you need to know the [____] behind it.

Make sure you can [____] your data collection method.

E.g. collecting the [____] of people in different [____] groups about a local [____]

Three [____] techniques:

① [____] — samples chosen at random.

② Systematic — samples taken at [____] intervals.

③ Stratified — samples taken from [____] to get good overall [____].

Data Presentation and Analysis

Describe your [____]:
- Spot patterns / correlations / [____].
- Compare [____].

Use [____] techniques, [____] and graphs to help.

You might be asked how [____] your [____] methods were.

Explain the [____]:
- Explain why [____] exist.
- Use geographical knowledge and [____].

Conclusion

[____] what the results show.

Answer the [____] question.

Explain:
- the [____].
- the [____] for the answer.
- how the [____] could be used [____] / [____] into the wider [____] world.

Evaluation

[____] what you did — [____] on:

Data collection [____]:
- [____] of data sets.
- [____] (unfairness).

Identify any [____] with your methods.

Data [____]:
- Did it [____] the question?
- Any other [____] data?

[____] of results:
- Any [____]?

ACCURATE RESULTS — very near [____] answer, [____] errors.

[____] of conclusions:
- Depends on reliability / [____] of results.

[____] RESULTS — can be [____].

[____] RESULTS — reliable and answer original [____].

Fieldwork

Data Collection

PRIMARY DATA —

SECONDARY DATA —

You start with a .... / .... — you need to know the ....

Make sure you can
....
....

E.g. collecting the .... of .... in .... age groups about a ....

Three sampling techniques:

1 **Random** — samples chosen

2 **Systematic** — samples taken

3 **Stratified** — samples taken

Data Presentation and Analysis

Describe
- Spot patterns /

- Compare

Use

Explain
- Explain
- Use geographical

You might be asked how
....
....
....
....
....

Conclusion

Summarise

Answer the original

Explain:
- the
- the evidence for
- how the results could be used

Evaluation

Assess what you did — comment on:

Data collection methods:
-
-

Identify ....
....
....
....

Data limitations:
- Did it

- Any

ACCURATE RESULTS —

Accuracy of results:
-

RELIABLE RESULTS — can be

Validity of conclusion:
- Depends

VALID RESULTS —

Geographical Applications

Maps

First Go:
..... / ..... / .....

Three Rules For Describing Distributions

1 Describe the _____ and _____ .

2 Make one _____ for each _____ available.

3 Use place _____ / _____ given.

If asked to _____ distribution, _____ it first.

Describing Locations

- Say _____ it is.
- Say what it's _____ .
- Use _____ .
- Use _____
  e.g. use ' _____ '
  instead of ' _____ '.

Latitude and Longitude — Global Coordinates

LATITUDE LINES — _____
lines measuring distance
or _____ of the _____

LONGITUDE LINES — _____
_____ lines measuring
distance or _____ of
the _____ .

_____ lines go _____ the globe.

120°W 60°W   60°E 120°E
       0°
60°N   60°N
30°N   30°N
0°   0°
30°S   30°S
60°S   60°S
120°W   0°   120°E
60°W 60°E

The Prime
Meridian runs
through
Greenwich, _____

Dot Maps

_____ dots show
_____ and _____ .

Location of factories

• = 10
factories

Proportional Symbol Maps

Larger symbols = _____ amounts

Car Parks in Drumshire

• 1
● 5
● 10

Cilden

Drange   Hove

Isolines

Isolines link _____ where something is the _____ .

E.g. Contours = same _____
    Isobars = same _____

Reading Isoline Maps:
- On a line → read off _____
- Between _____ lines → _____ .

Completing Isoline Maps:
- Join _____ with the same _____
- Never _____ other isolines.

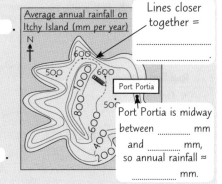

Average annual rainfall on
Itchy Island (mm per year)

N

600
500   600
Port Portia
500

Lines closer
together = _____
....
....

Port Portia is midway
between .... mm
and .... mm,
so annual rainfall ≈
.... mm.

Maps

Three Rules For Describing Distributions

1 Describe the

2 Make one point for

3 Use

If asked to explain distribution, ...

Describing Locations

- Say
- Say
- Use
- Use

Latitude and Longitude — Global Coordinates

LATITUDE LINES —

LONGITUDE LINES —

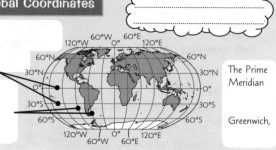

The Prime
Meridian

Greenwich,

Dot Maps

Identical dots show

Location of factories

• = 10 factories

Proportional Symbol Maps

☐ = ☐

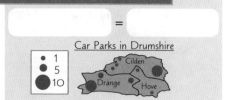

Car Parks in Drumshire

• 1
• 5
● 10

Isolines

Isolines link places

E.g.

Reading Isoline Maps:
- On
- Between

Completing Isoline Maps:
- Join
- Never

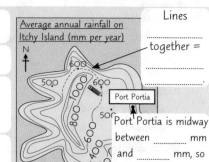

Average annual rainfall on
Itchy Island (mm per year)

Port Portia

Lines
....
→ together =
....
....

Port Portia is midway
between .... mm
and .... mm, so
annual ....
≈ .... mm.

Maps

First Go:
..... / ..... / .....

Choropleth Maps

Show _____ using _____ or patterns.

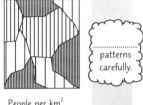

_____ patterns carefully.

People per km²
☐ = 0 — 99
⫼ = 100 — 199
⫼ = 200+

Flow Lines

Arrows show _____.

Arrow widths can show _____.

E.g. about _____ as many people come to the _____ from the _____ than from the _____

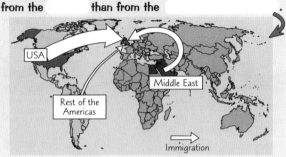

USA

Middle East

Rest of the Americas

➡ Immigration

Desire Lines

- Show journeys between _____.
- Straight — _____ roads.
- One line = one _____.

These are used to show _____ people _____ to get to a _____, e.g. a shop, and _____ they've _____.

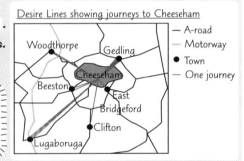

Desire Lines showing journeys to Cheeseham

Woodthorpe
Gedling
Cheeseham
Beeston
East Bridgeford
Clifton
Lugaboruga

— A-road
— Motorway
● Town
— One journey

Ordnance Survey (OS®) Symbols

▰▰ Motorway
▬ Main (A) road
═ Secondary (B) road
� Railway
— Railway
–·– County boundary
National Park boundaries

☐ Building
⬥ _____
------ _____
🔆 _____
ℹ Tourist information centre
P _____
+ ▮ ▮ _____

Compass Points

North
NW
West
SE

Remember: _____
Eat _____ Wheat.

Geographical Skills

Second Go:
..... /..... /.....

Maps

Choropleth Maps

Show

People per km²

| = 0 — 99

||| = 100 — 199

▦ = 200+

Flow Lines

Arrows
Arrow widths
E.g. about twice as many people from the USA than

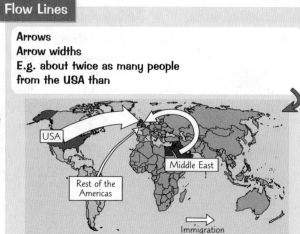

USA

Rest of the Americas

Middle East

Immigration

Desire Lines

• **Show**

• **Straight —**
• **One line =**

These are used to show ....
....
....
.... and where they've come from.

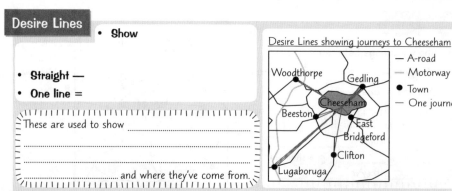

Desire Lines showing journeys to Cheeseham

— A-road
— Motorway
● Town
— One journey

Woodthorpe   Gedling

Beeston   Cheeseham

East Bridgeford

Clifton

Lugaboruga

Ordnance Survey (OS®) Symbols

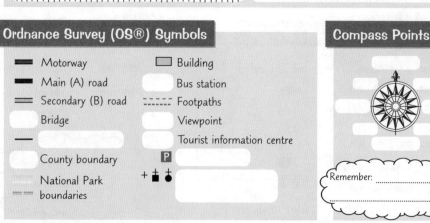

Motorway

Main (A) road

Secondary (B) road

Bridge

—

County boundary

National Park boundaries

Building

Bus station

Footpaths

Viewpoint

Tourist information centre

P

+ ☩ ●

Compass Points

Remember: ....

Geographical Skills

Maps

Grid References

Across value = ... Up value = ...

Four Figure:

- First _____ figures = value for _____ edge of square.
- Last _____ figures = value for _____ edge of square.

Six Figure:

- _____ square into _____ across and up.
- First _____ figures = value for _____ edge of _____ and number of tenths _____.
- Last _____ figures = value for _____ of square and number of _____ up.

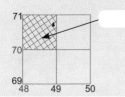

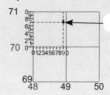

Two Steps to Find a Distance

1 Measure _____ on map.

2 Compare _____ to _____.

Scale 1:50 000
2 centimetres to 1 kilometre (one grid square)
Kilometres

1.1 km apart

2.2 lined up with O on scale.

Contours and Spot Heights

Contour lines join points of _____.

Height above _____ level / altitude (___)

Lines _____
_____
= steeper slope

_____ (trig)
— _____ point in area (m).

_____ height

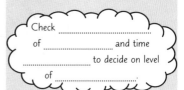

Sketching Maps

- Use a _____.
- Copy the _____.
- Get main _____ right.
- Measure _____ points.
- Add _____.

Check .... of .... and time .... to decide on level of ....

Geographical Skills

Maps

Grid References

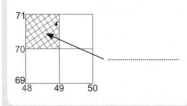

.... value = ... value = ...

Four Figure:

- First two figures =

- Last two figures =

....

Six Figure:

- Divide squares into

- First three figures = value

- Last three figures =

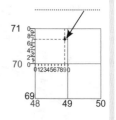

Two Steps to Find a Distance

1

2.2 cm

2

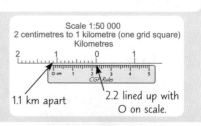

Scale 1:50 000
2 centimetres to 1 kilometre (one grid square)
Kilometres

1.1 km apart

2.2 lined up with O on scale.

Contours and Spot Heights

Contour lines

Height

Lines

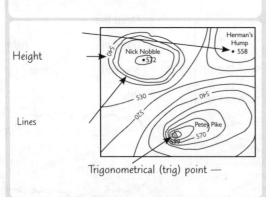

Trigonometrical (trig) point —

Sketching Maps

- **Use**

- **Copy**

- **Get**

- **Measure**

- **Add**

Check ....

of ....

....

....

Charts and Graphs

Bar Charts

1. To _____ bar charts:
   Find _____ of bar. ➡ Go to _____ . ➡ Read _____ .

2. To read divided bar charts:
   Find top and _____   Read _____
   _____ of relevant ➡ _____ ➡ bottom
   _____ of bar.   off scale.   from top.

3. To complete bar charts:
   Find number on ➡ Trace line across ➡ Use _____
   _____ scale.   to _____ of _____ .   to draw bar.

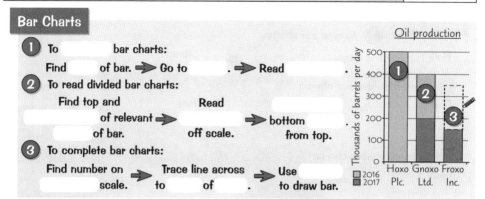

Oil production

Thousands of barrels per day

Hoxo Plc. / Gnoxo Ltd. / Froxo Inc.

2016 / 2017

Histograms

Use histograms for _____
divided into _____ .

Draw and plot them like _____
but remember to check bar _____ .

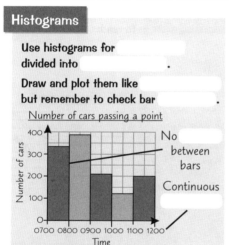

Number of cars passing a point

Number of cars / Time

No _____ between bars

Continuous _____

Line Graphs

To read: Find _____ on one _____ .
Read _____ or up to _____ ,
then read value off _____ .

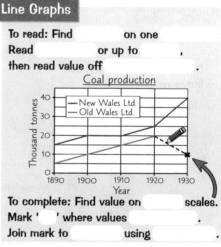

Coal production

New Wales Ltd.
Old Wales Ltd.

Thousand tonnes / Year

To complete: Find value on _____ scales.
Mark ' ' where values _____ .
Join mark to _____ using _____ .

Scatter Graphs

Scatter graphs show the _____
_____ between two things.

To read: Look at graph's _____ / _____ &
how _____ points are to line of best fit.
Close to line → _____ correlation.
Far from line → _____ correlation.

To _____ points:
Find value on _____ scales
and _____ where they _____ .

To draw line of best fit, draw _____ through _____ of scattered points.

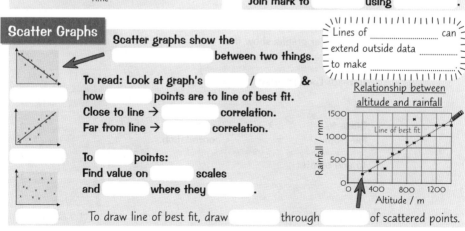

Lines of _____ can extend outside data _____ to make _____

Relationship between altitude and rainfall

Rainfall / mm / Altitude / m

Line of best fit

Geographical Skills

Charts and Graphs

Bar Charts

1 To read bar charts:

Find ➡ Go ➡ Read

2 To read divided bar charts:

Find ➡ Read ➡ Subtract

3 To complete bar charts:

Find ➡ Trace ➡ Use

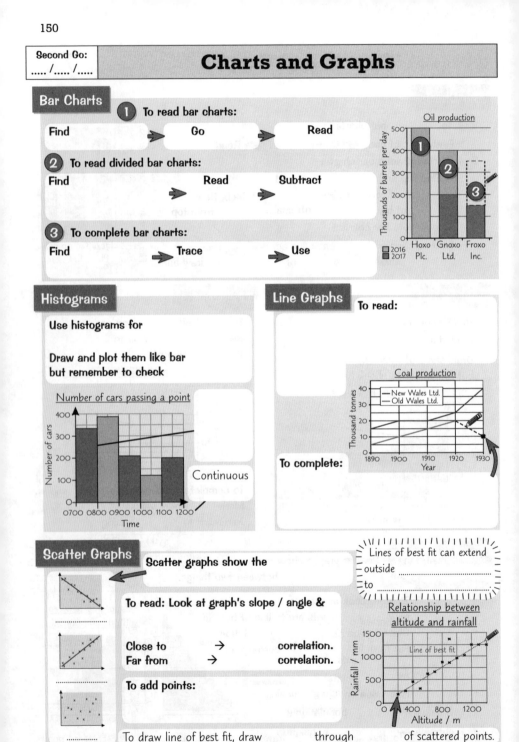

Oil production

Thousands of barrels per day

① ② ③

☐ 2016 ■ 2017

Hoxo Plc. | Gnoxo Ltd. | Froxo Inc.

Histograms

Use histograms for

Draw and plot them like bar but remember to check

Number of cars passing a point

Number of cars

0700 0800 0900 1000 1100 1200
Time

Continuous

Line Graphs

To read:

Coal production

— New Wales Ltd.
— Old Wales Ltd.

Thousand tonnes

1890 1900 1910 1920 1930
Year

To complete:

Scatter Graphs

Scatter graphs show the

Lines of best fit can extend outside .... to ....

To read: Look at graph's slope / angle &

Close to → .... correlation.
Far from → .... correlation.

To add points:

Relationship between altitude and rainfall

Rainfall / mm

Line of best fit

0 400 800 1200
Altitude / m

To draw line of best fit, draw .... through .... of scattered points.

 ✓ ✓ 🙂 ✓

Charts and Graphs

Pie Charts

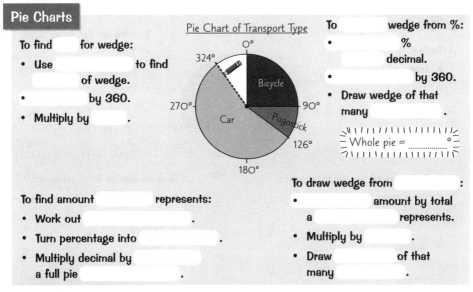

To find _____ for wedge:
- Use _____ to find _____ of wedge.
- _____ by 360.
- Multiply by _____.

Pie Chart of Transport Type

To _____ wedge from %:
- _____ %
- _____ decimal.
- _____ by 360.
- Draw wedge of that many _____.

Whole pie = ...°

To find amount _____ represents:
- Work out _____.
- Turn percentage into _____.
- Multiply decimal by a full pie _____.

To draw wedge from _____:
- _____ amount by total a _____ represents.
- Multiply by _____.
- Draw _____ of that many _____.

Dispersion Diagrams

Cross between _____ chart and _____ chart.

- _____ of data goes on one _____.
- _____ goes on the other.

.... dots in ....
= event more ....

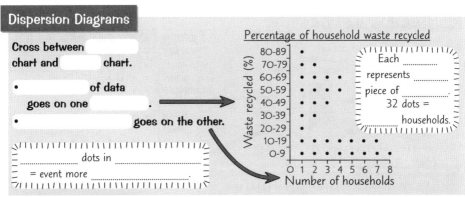

Percentage of household waste recycled

Each .... represents .... piece of .... 32 dots = ... households.

Waste recycled (%)
80-89, 70-79, 60-69, 50-59, 40-49, 30-39, 20-29, 10-19, 0-9

Number of households

Population Pyramids

Show the population of a _____ by _____ and _____.

- _____ axis — no. of people
- _____ axis — age groups
- Left side — _____ population
- Right side — _____ population

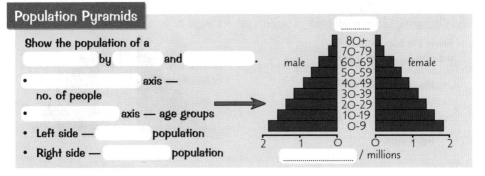

male   female

80+, 70-79, 60-69, 50-59, 40-49, 30-39, 20-29, 10-19, 0-9

.... / millions

Geographical Skills

Charts and Graphs

Pie Charts

To find % for wedge:
- Use

- Divide
-

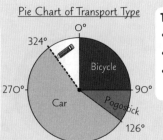

Pie Chart of Transport Type

0°
324°
Bicycle
270°
90°
Car
Pogostick
126°
180°

To draw wedge from %:
- Turn
- Multiply
- Draw

.... = 360°

To find amount wedge represents:
- Work out
- Turn

- Multiply

To draw wedge from amount:
- Divide

- Multiply
- Draw

Dispersion Diagrams

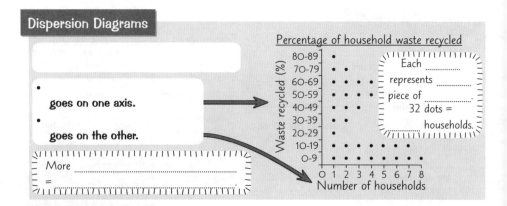

- goes on one axis.
- goes on the other.

More ....
=

Percentage of household waste recycled

Waste recycled (%)

80-89
70-79
60-69
50-59
40-49
30-39
20-29
10-19
0-9

0 1 2 3 4 5 6 7 8
Number of households

Each .... represents .... piece of .... 32 dots = ... households.

Population Pyramids

Show the population of a country by age and gender.

- Horizontal axis —
- Vertical axis —
- Left side —
- Right side —

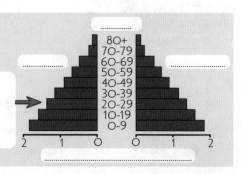

80+
70-79
60-69
50-59
40-49
30-39
20-29
10-19
0-9

2   1   0   0   1   2

....

Statistics

Definitions

Mode, median and mean = ...

MODE
The _____ _____ number.

MEDIAN
The _____ value (when in _____ order).

MEAN
The _____ of items ÷ _____ of items. ➡ 798 ÷ 7 = 114

e.g. 64   64   90   95   142   159   184

When there are _____ middle numbers, the median is _____ the _____.

RANGE
The difference between the _____ and _____ number. ➡ 184 − 64 = 120

LOWER QUARTILE
The value a _____ of the way through the _____ data.

UPPER QUARTILE
The value _____ of the way through the _____ data.

e.g. 2   3   6   6   7   9   13   14   17   22   22

INTERQUARTILE RANGE
The difference between the _____ and the _____. ➡ 17 − 6 = 11

Percentages and Percentage Change

To find **X** as a _____ of Y:

1 Divide _____ by _____.

2 _____ this number by _____.

E.g. This year, 35 out of 270 houses in Oldtown were burgled. Calculate the % of houses that were burgled.

To find 35 as a percentage of 270:

To calculate percentage _____:

$$\text{percentage change} = \frac{_____ - \text{original value}}{_____} \times _____$$

E.g. Last year, only 24 houses were burgled. Calculate the percentage change in burglaries. ➡

A positive value shows an _____

A negative value shows a _____

Geographical Skills

Statistics

Definitions

_____ = ...

MODE:

MEDIAN:

MEAN:

➡ 798 ÷ 7 = 114

e.g. 64   64   90   95   142   159   184

When there are two middle numbers, the ....

RANGE:

➡ 184 − 64 = 120

LOWER QUARTILE:

UPPER QUARTILE:

MEDIAN

e.g. 2   3   6   6   7   9   13   14   17   22   22

INTERQUARTILE RANGE:

➡ 17 − 6 = 11

Percentages and Percentage Change

To find X as a percentage of Y:

1

2

E.g. This year, **35 out of 270** houses in Oldtown were burgled. Calculate the % of houses that were burgled.

To find 35 as a percentage of 270:

To calculate percentage change:

percentage change = $\dfrac{............. \text{value} − .... \text{value}}{.............} \times ....$

....
....
....
....
....

E.g. Last year, only **24 houses** were burgled. Calculate the percentage change in burglaries.

Mixed Practice Quizzes

Here's one final set of quizzes based on p.141-154 to map your progress, then you're free to scatter. Go grab a percentage of pie to celebrate if you want — I mean it.

Quiz 1 | Date: ...... / ...... / ......

1) What three rules do you need to remember when describing distributions? ✓
2) How do you find the percentage for a wedge on a pie chart? ✓
3) Give two things you should consider when assessing your data collection methods for your fieldwork. ✓
4) What does each dot represent on a dispersion diagram? ✓
5) How do you add a point to a line graph? ✓
6) What is the difference between primary data and secondary data? ✓
7) How do you find the interquartile range for a set of data? ✓
8) Name two ways in which choropleth maps can show variation. ✓
9) Name three different measures of average. ✓
10) What do isolines do? Give an example of a type of isoline. ✓

Total:

Quiz 2 | Date: ...... / ...... / ......

1) What is the difference between latitude lines and longitude lines? ✓
2) Name three different sampling techniques. ✓
3) True or false? Lines of best fit can help you make predictions. ✓
4) Give two things that you should do when describing locations. ✓
5) Is a four figure or a six figure grid reference more useful when locating a specific location on a map? Why? ✓
6) What is the difference between an 'easting' and a 'northing'? ✓
7) What should the degrees in a completed pie chart add up to? ✓
8) What two things can the arrows in flow line maps show? ✓
9) When calculating percentage change, what does a positive value show? ✓
10) Is a scatter graph with points that make it very difficult to draw a line of best fit more likely to have 'positive', 'negative' or 'no' correlation? ✓

Total:

Geographical Skills

Mixed Practice Quizzes

Quiz 3   Date: ...... / ...... / ......

1) True or false? On proportional symbol maps,
   larger symbols represent larger amounts.

2) Describe the correlation of a scatter graph that
   has points which are close to the line of best fit.

3) What is the difference between accurate and reliable results?

4) What does a population pyramid show?

5) What affects the validity of results?

6) How would you calculate the mean for a set of data?

7) State two things that the conclusion of your fieldwork should explain.

8) How would you find X as a percentage of Y?

9) What do desire lines show?

10) How do you work out the distance between two places on a map?

Total:

Quiz 4   Date: ...... / ...... / ......

1) True or false? Both histograms and bar charts have gaps between the bars.

2) Suggest a rhyme that you could use to remember
   the four main points on a compass.

3) What do dot maps show?

4) What is the formula for calculating percentage change?

5) a) Give two things you could do to describe data
   collected as part of a geographical enquiry.
   b) Now give two things you should do when explaining your results.

6) What goes on each axis of a dispersion diagram?

7) A contour map has lines that are spaced very far apart.
   Describe the gradient of the area that would be shown by this contour map.

8) Give four important things to remember when drawing a map.

9) How do you work out a six figure grid reference?

10) What is a 'trigonometrical point' and what does it show on a map?

Total:

Camouflage Champions

Hard-working geographers captured the images below during their travels around the world. They show some of Mother Nature's most cunningly disguised creatures, but many animals' secret haunts remain undocumented — keep your eyes peeled.

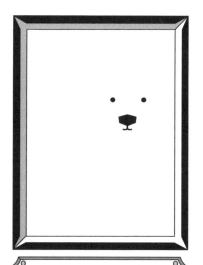

'Polar Bear in a Snowstorm'
by B. Link & E. Scon

'Zebra at a Refereeing Convention'
by R. U. C. Ingdis

'Dalmatian on a Pebble Beach'
by Husag Uudboy

'Snake Amongst the Shoelaces'
by Watt Jurstep

158

Acknowledgements

Data for causes of deforestation in the Amazon on page 31 and 32 from Mongabay.com.

Topographic map of the United Kingdom on page 49 and 50 by Captain Blood, Licensed under the Creative Commons Attribution-Share Alike 3.0 Unported license. https://creativecommons.org/licenses/by-sa/3.0/deed. en)

Photo on page 53 and 54 (Old Harry Rock) © Raymond Knapman. Licensed under the Creative Commons Attribution-Share Alike 2.0 Generic Licence. http://creativecommons.org/licenses/by-sa/2.0/

Photo on page 55 and 56 (aerial view of Alkborough Flats, 2007) © Chris. Licensed under the Creative Commons Attribution-Share Alike 2.0 Generic Licence. http://creativecommons.org/licenses/by-sa/2.0/

Data on the Oxford Flood Alleviation Scheme on page 69 and 70 © Crown copyright. Contains public sector information licensed under the Open Government Licence v3.0. https://www.nationalarchives.gov.uk/doc/open-government-licence/version/3/

Urban population data on page 81 and 82 source: United Nations Population Division. World Population Prospects: 2018 Revision. From The World Bank: World Development Indicators, licensed under the CC BY-4.0 License. https://creativecommons.org/licenses/by/4.0/

Birth rate data on page 81 and 82 source:
(1) United Nations Population Division. World Population Prospects: 2017 Revision.
(2) Census reports and other statistical publications from national statistical offices,
(3) Eurostat: Demographic Statistics,
(4) United Nations Statistical Division. Population and Vital Statistics Report (various years),
(5) U.S. Census Bureau: International Database, and
(6) Secretariat of the Pacific Community: Statistics and Demography Programme. From The World Bank: World Development Indicators, licensed under the CC BY-4.0 License. https://creativecommons.org/licenses/by/4.0/

Map symbols on pages 145-148 © Crown copyright and database rights 2020 OS 100034841

Every effort has been made to locate copyright holders and obtain permission to reproduce sources. For those sources where it has been difficult to trace the copyright holder of the work, we would be grateful for information. If any copyright holder would like us to make an amendment to the acknowledgements, please notify us and we will gladly update the book at the next reprint. Thank you.